MY TIMESHARE INSIDER

Timeshare
Tips & Tricks

Timeshare Tips & Tricks

Stay at five star resorts for pennies, eliminate maintenance costs, trade, what to do when you don't want it anymore.

By VINCENT LEHR
©2011 SIG LLC. All rights reserved.

ISBN-13: 978-1456368913
ISBN-10: 1456368915
LCCN: 2011907169
CreateSpace, North Charleston, South Carolina

Dedication

This is Dedicated to my lovely wife who stands by me through everything I do and helps us to accomplish our dreams with God, love and laughter.

Forward by James W. Pickens

Dear Reader,
This book is important. For over thirty-five years I have been sharing with sales professionals around the world the exact values and obligations they owe to their customers. In the sales industry today as in the past there are too many sales people who simply want to sell their product to someone and immediately forget them after the transaction is closed. This conduct and attitude is not and should not be tolerated. Customers come first and that is a basic given in sales philosophy that can never be changed.

The timesharing business is a rewarding and fascinating venture not only for customers, and owners but for sales people as well. This unique step in vacationing and travel has come a long way from when it was first introduced in the early seventies in the United States. In fact timesharing actually started around 1955 when five Austrian dentists co-owned a chalet in Switzerland. They, in their wisdom, decided to share different weeks in the ski chalet with their families so their costs could be shared with each other, thus making owning and maintaining the chalet more financially comfortable for each family. The word timesharing itself comes from computer people. For example in the 1950's only a handful of companies had computers. These large and bulky electrical units were usually housed in the basement of a corporation's home office. When the computers were not in use, the company that owned the computer would let other companies, for a fee, use them. Thus, the word "timeshare" came.

Reader it is the duty of every sales person on this earth to tell the truth, to respect, love and understand their customers. This manual written by Vinnie Lehr fulfills that duty, because he explains timesharing and all of its integral parts in a way all can understand and utilize. I have never written a foreword or endorsement for another author in my entire career, but Vinnie, besides being a personal friend of many years, has put down on paper the truth about how timeshare works, how timeshares are exchanged, and what to look out for and avoid in the timeshare market place. This little book will save you many hours of research, worry, and sleeplessness due to unanswered questions regarding your time share, membership, points, or general concerns. In the years I've known Vinnie Lehr; I have never seen him take a customer for granted. He has always demonstrated integrity and treated each customer like one of his family members. Vinnie wrote this book to educate every timeshare owner, and potential owner on the big or little points a salesperson might have left out of his or her presentation. This timeshare study and effort will not only explain in detail everything an owner needs to know but will direct and outline ways to save money and not be taken advantage of.

Again this book is important. Customers need to know the truth about timeshare and/or travel clubs and they need to understand exactly why certain companies do this or that. This book has the answers and for me knowing the timesharing business from the inside out, it's about time. This manual is overdue and I'm proud of its contents and author. May you, the reader take full advantage of your timeshare, enjoy every minute and relax knowing there are good sales people out there who honorably look after your interest and those people in time will turn into friends you'll cherish forever. So please rest easy, understand your purchase and travel. Let the world know you exist and share your personality with everyone you meet.

Most respectfully,
James W Pickens

Table of Contents

Introduction

Why timeshare is great

My name is Vinnie Lehr, and I have been in the timeshare industry for nearly a decade. I have been involved in nearly every aspect of the industry, from resale's to booking tours on the main drag of Sedona Arizona. As a sales professional in the industry I have worked with the biggest names in timeshare, such as Wyndham, Diamond Resorts, Bluegreen, Geo Resorts, and Monarch Grand Vacations.

After working in the industry, learning the products, staying at the resorts, and listening to thousands of owners, I have learned nearly every aspect of ownership. I decided to write this book to help out individuals who own timeshares and those who don't know what to do with their timeshares once they have ceased their usefulness. This is also a how-to guide for how to best use your timeshare and get the most value out of it. I will give you ideas on everything from offsetting your maintenance fees, to trading your property to a five-star resort, to getting multiple weeks out of every one week you own. I will teach you how to navigate through the resale world or make money with your property by renting it out when you are not using it. If you want to turn your timeshare into a business, you will learn the things the developers will never tell you.

For specific information on your particular situation or for anything I have not covered in this book, please visit my website at www.mytimeshareinsider.com and we can assist you further. In order to make this a book that people will actually read, I have tried to condense the information and cover the questions most owners ask. If you have any questions or specific situations, which is very likely, again, feel free to contact my offices and we can assist you in any way or do any research on your behalf that is necessary to help you.

There are three major things I would like to cover in this book:

1. **Trading**

2. **Renting**

3. **Offsetting your maintenance**

I believe that as a timeshare owner you should do your best to offset your maintenance costs, get multiple weeks out of one, and stay at five-star resorts whenever possible. If you can do these things consistently, a timeshare is a great investment that cuts your costs to lower than they would be if you bought vacations online, no matter what the discount.

Timeshare have provided millions of people with above-average family vacation experiences they might not have otherwise been able to accomplish. I have seen owners create memories with their families that most people could only dream of. The entire purpose of timeshare is to allow people the ability to stay at high quality resorts without paying hundreds of dollars per night, but a vacation ownership package is not the least expensive way to go unless you know how to use it. The majority of people, in my estimation, do not use their programs effectively or don't use them at all.

Vacation ownership allows people who might not normally afford to take a high quality vacation a chance to live like they're rich when they do travel. The timeshare industry was started in the1960's in the French Alps for Europeans who took holidays. A standard holiday in Europe is when you take an entire month off of work to spend with your family. In fact, in some places in Europe you are disqualified from some insurance if you do not take at least three weeks of vacation. Continuously working without taking a break can lead to high stress levels that increase your odds of heart disease, cancer, divorce and general unhappiness. Vacation ownership is a way to prepay your vacations for a lifetime with a one-time purchase price. After that, your cost is only an annual maintenance fee, and you can go on frequent vacations at high quality resorts.

As I write this, I am sitting at my desk in a nearly full resort in the middle of the worst economic time since the Great Depression. Even people who are on unemployment are still traveling because their vacations have been prepaid. When people are already paying for something, they tend to use it more to justify spending their money.

Timeshares have evolved over the last few decades to meet the needs of a wide variety of people. Currently, there are over five million people who own some sort of vacation ownership package from some of the biggest companies in the world. Most timeshare resorts are located in popular destination areas with nearly every major developer now involved. Every major hotel company– including Four Seasons, Hilton, Wyndham, Disney, Berkley group, Sheraton, Westin and many others–has a timeshare program to offer. These companies have developed programs to allow you to do everything from staying at campgrounds to staying on private catamarans in the Bahamas. You can enjoy cruises, all-inclusive resorts, and vacation houses all with your program. Some companies have even started buying property on the moon for their owners to use, eventually.

With timeshares, you are not just staying in a hotel room; you are staying in a fully furnished condo typically twice the size of an average hotel room with all of the amenities of home. One of the cost-saving features is the kitchen because it allows you to eat meals in your room. The rooms also provide you a homier feel because of the living rooms and extra bedrooms which provide extra comfort. Some people say they just use the room to sleep in, but I can guarantee they have never stayed at a Westin Presidential Unit in Hawaii for a small $180 exchange fee.

No matter where you own, you have the option of using any of several exchange companies to trade to thousands of resorts on every continent in any desirable location on the planet. If you utilize your timeshare correctly, you can stay at a five-star resort where people pay thousands of dollars per week for pennies on the dollar.

The key is to know how to use your timeshare effectively and have ways to offset your maintenance costs. I have written this book as an informative guide on how to use your program no matter which company you own with or what you want to do with it. When you own a vacation program, you have many options. In addition to staying at high-end properties, you can use it as a rental to make money, contribute it as a charitable donation, or leave it as a legacy to your family. In life families can change with having children or getting divorced. Unexpected things like loss of income can also occur. When those things happen, a lot of individuals do not know what to do with their timeshares. This book will give you options on what you can do with a timeshare for any type of situation. Neither the developers nor the sales agents are there to help you past the sale. That is where this book and I come in.

I don't want to make this book just a big ad for my business, but we have developed a company where you can call and speak with a real person who has an interest in helping you with advice rather than just trying to sell you something. It seems everyone out there has a hidden agenda to try and sell you what they want you to buy not exactly what you need. I have written this book and started my company to assist owners while navigating through these sometimes complex topics. Of course I charge a fee to support myself and my family but I have no affiliations or loyalties to any particular company. The reason I am writing this book under a surname is because I am still in the industry and I doubt they would be thrilled with me revealing a lot of the alternative options you have in this industry to buy, sell, rent or trade.

My mission with this book and my company is not to make everyone rich, but to give advice you can count on without the fear that someone is taking advantage of you. My company charges very little for safe and sound advice and we believe we will be rewarded for our efforts. We do charge a small month's fee for the advice that I will lay out in this book. If you require further assistance or would like to speak with me personally, we would be more than happy to have you as a member and we will work hard to assist you with anything you may need.

Finally, you get the knowledge you need and the help you want!

Chapter One

What kinds of programs are there?

As timeshare has evolved over the years, there have been many innovations and new programs from various companies. This has created what is now called the "Vacation ownership industry," which provides vacation plans from all the major developers in the world. Most of these companies own hotel chains as well as ownership resorts. The vacation ownership industry is now a $6 billion industry with over six million owners worldwide.

What kind of program you buy and with which company is completely up to you and what you are looking for in your life. There are traditional timeshares, fractional, point systems, and travel clubs, all of which have certain benefits for different types of people. The most popular timeshares in the early days were deeded fixed weeks in high (popular) destination areas. As needs advanced, companies came up with floating time, you can use your unit anytime throughout the year. Eventually, the points program revolutionized the industry. Nowadays, you can utilize your credits over and over for all forms of vacations, from houseboats to country cottages, cruises, all-inclusive packages, adventure packages, private yachts, five-star resorts, and everything in between. Due to the ever-changing needs of vacationers and the need to increase business revenue, developers have made changes to their programs, allowing owners to access nearly anything they want. These innovations in ownership programs allow timeshare owners to spend their money once and redeem the benefits year after year, saving thousands and thousands of dollars.

If you are reading this book, then most likely you have a timeshare of some kind. Each kind has different rules for booking and renting as well as which types of tax deductions you are eligible to take. In traditional timeshare, you are buying a certain deeded week at a resort for a definite time of the year. While these weeks provide advantages for people looking to stay at the same place every year at the same time, it can be a little restrictive compared to the points programs. The benefits of deeded timeshares are that there are a few tax deductions you can take as well as guarantee yourself a reservation for the week you own every year. These types of ownerships have evolved by allowing you to use floating time anytime of the year as well as lock off the units or split the week up in some cases.

Most likely if you are a timeshare owner you know what type of ownership you have; however, after being in the business, I realize there are still a lot of people that don't know what they own or how much of it they do own. So, for the sake of the book, and in case you have questions about the programs, I will give a brief explanation of the different types of programs now available.

One of the most popular programs, and the one that started the industry, is **deeded fixed weeks**. These increments of time have all the same rights as a regular piece of real estate such as usage, the ability to rent, the option to donate or give it away and the right to resell it to another person. If you have bought one of these weeks, you would have been issued a specific week number in a specific condo at a particular resort. Deeded weeks are great as far as getting specific times of the year, stability, and a few extra tax benefits that the other timeshares owners do not get. For the purpose of this book, I will refer to these as "traditional" weeks or units.

There are also **leasehold deeded weeks,** which you typically find in other countries. These have the same rights as a deeded week. However, after a period of time- usually thirty years- the rights revert back to the developer. Occasionally, these are offered in perpetuity, but many do not convey ownership of the land, merely the apartment or unit of the accommodation.

With **right to use,** you can use the timeshare in accordance with the contract, but at some point the contract ends and all rights revert back to the property owner or developer. Most people who own units in Mexico have this type of program. The only downside to leases is that a company owns the reservation system, and the owners are not in control. In these cases, the rights of use may be lost by the demise of the company or at the whim of a foreign government. In this book we will consider these as "traditional" timeshares as well.

Within the deeded weeks there are **fixed weeks** as well as, **floating weeks**. The fixed weeks are great if you bought a good week, but not so good if you did not. Floating weeks are good because even if you did not buy a great week, you still have the ability to get one if you put in for it early enough. In most cases, the holiday weeks are sold as fixed weeks. Floating weeks give owners a chance for a good week but not much flexibility for anything else. I will still refer to all of these weeks above as traditional weeks.

The fastest growing and most popular vacation ownership programs are **vacation clubs**. These programs are typically sold as either non-deeded or with rights in perpetuity. With some of these vacation clubs, you may own units in multiple resorts in different locations. A few of these clubs consist only of a few individual weeks at other developers' resorts. This allows the companies to offer many locations, but you really do not own anything except for time. These club developers can lose inventory at resorts you bought into in the blink of an eye. Developers like GEO Holiday have this particular type of system, which gives you many properties to choose from, but they can lose the properties and leave you with nowhere to go.

One of the newest and most innovative ways of selling ownership is a **points system**. Most Americans unfortunately do not travel as much as they do in Europe and while working hard is not a bad thing and we are by far extremely productive, we all would benefit from more travel.

Most of the larger companies such as Wyndham, Starwood, Hilton, Marriott, and several others, have switched their programs to the points system to give added value to their programs as well as give owners the ability to have maximum flexibility. Points systems allow owners to call anywhere from two years in advance down to the day before check-in. Points allow you the ability to stay in any size room, from a studio to a penthouse, on any day of the week for any length of time. Points memberships allow owners maximum savings by allowing you to travel in off times of the year as well as during the week, giving you the ability to increase your number of vacation days. You have the ability to book multiple units simultaneously at multiple locations in various rooms for as long as you have credits. This provides a tremendous advantage over older timeshares, where if you book a reservation you must stay at the same time of the year at the same place.

Points systems are for busy people who cannot go on vacation for long periods of time. They are also great for people who like to do different things, as well as stay in different resorts. Points owners are issued the number of credits they buy annually and can use them any way they would like inside the resort group. Most points programs are associated with large resort groups offering a broad selection of options for destinations. These systems also give you the ability to use your points for airlines, car rentals, tour packages, house-boats, RV parks, cruises, activities, and even gift cards. While I personally believe these are the best way to go, it is up to you to make that decision. In subsequent chapters I will give you more of my thoughts on which types of programs you should buy and which ones to stay away from.

Points programs offer maximum flexibility, as you can stay at any resort in the inventory without an external exchange fee. With points, you can stay as long as you want, when you want, in whatever size accommodations you want, provided you have enough points and the reservations are available. Some of these things are possible with deeded weeks, but they are more difficult to do and take expertise. The only things that affect points owners are the popularity of the resort, size of the room, number of nights, season, and the specific nights needed. With a points system, you have the ability to work the system to your advantage and maximize your vacation time. For the purpose of this book, I will refer to the points system as **point's week**. If you know what you are doing, you can potentially get up to four weeks of time out of one week's worth of points, compared to a maximum of two weeks with a deeded property.

Whatever type of property you own or are thinking of buying, you really can get a lot of use and value out of it if you understand how to use it correctly. If you do not take advantage of the timeshare benefits on a continuous basis, then a timeshare is a big waste of money, especially if you financed it for a long period of time.

Timeshare is not the cheapest way to vacation by any means, especially with all of the travel websites available. You absolutely must know how to utilize your program properly. If you have $50,000 to $100,000 cash to buy a timeshare, most likely you are better off putting that money into a great investment and putting the maintenance money you would spend into the same account so you can compound the interest. If you do this, I am sure that when you retire you will have enough money to go wherever you want to go. However, most people do not have that luxury of initial investment capital. For the rest of us, utilizing a vacation ownership package to stay at nice resorts is a more feasible option. As for staying at hotels off internet travel sites, that's all well and good as well as very reasonably priced. I even do that from time to time. However, many people have families and are past the college phase of sleeping six to a room and leaving the next morning. Many people would like to stay in a wonderful five-star resort; but, do not have the money to do so. I hear these excuses all the time:

"I do not go on vacation to stay in the room."

"We are always out doing things on our trip."

"It's just the two of us; we do not need much room."

"We are only staying for a few days."

"I don't care about having a nice room."

"I don't feel comfortable at a nice place. I am just a simple person."

"Those places cost too much."

"It's not worth the extra money to stay in a nice place."

"I never travel with friends or family."

Now, money is not everything, and you do not have to stay at the Four Seasons to have a great time. I know that full well; however, I also know if you won the lottery you would not be staying at a Super 8 hotel off of the side of the freeway, either. If you inherited money, you would not be taking a two-day cruise to Mexico in a room next to the broiler room or staying at the La Quinta. Just this year, I stayed at the Ritz Carlton at Lake Las Vegas–one of the best resorts in Las Vegas–as well as the Best Western in Lone Pine California. The difference in cost was very small compared to a timeshare. Let me tell you, the trip to the Ritz was a lot more memorable than the one to the Best Western. So, for all of you who use these excuses now, I will teach you how to stay at five-star resorts for the same price as that Super 8 motel every year. I know that, yes, you are out on the town a lot on vacation, but you are still sleeping in the room, showering, resting and everything else.

So, no matter what your status in life, the poor Mexican writing this book is going to show you how to expand your horizons, increase your quality of vacations, and make a better life for yourself.

Ninety percent of your memories come from ten percent of your experiences. I am going to teach you how you and your family can have an above-average vacation for pennies on the dollar for the rest of your life. If you see a chubby Mexican on the beach writing a book at the Four Seasons, stop and say hi, because it will most likely be me.

Chapter Two

How to get the best use of your timeshare as well as the reservations you actually want

Nearly all timeshare owners have difficulties making the reservations they want, when they would most like to go. They give up and think their ownership does not work well. My synopsis of vacation ownership is this: you got a nice gift to go tour a resort; you then spent thousands of dollars; then, the company slapped you on the butt and said "Have fun."

Most companies do not properly train you on how to actually use what you bought in various situations. Without training, people continuously cannot get what they want and end up losing their points or time while still paying all of the fees. Owners can go years without using their programs while paying thousands of dollars, and many have no idea what options are available to them. If you go to the resorts to get help, you end up with a salesperson who tells you the only way to fix it is to buy more of what you already have. In many cases, there is some truth to that; however, knowing how to utilize the system will yield the resorts you are looking for.

One of the biggest complaints is the lack of ability to get into resorts in high destination areas when it is convenient for you. A majority of owners have problems booking reservations on short notice in places they would "actually" want to go to. You may find you cannot use your units every year, and the options of what to do are very limited or not well known. Even when you actually know what you want to do, you might call and talk to someone who makes it seem so difficult that you decide to pay cash for another room, defeating the purpose of ownership.

You might also like to do other, more non-traditional, types of trips, which you may believe are unavailable to you or your program. Even after you finally get a reservation, you may find that a lot of the resorts are not kept up as well as they should be for the amount of maintenance they charge.

This chapter will cover the general procedures for making reservations properly, taking into consideration both deeded and points weeks. If you follow my advice, you will get more reservations when you want them and where you want them, as well as doubling or tripling your time at the properties you choose. Just as with everything else in life, it is good to know someone on the "inside."

I have not worked at all sixty vacation ownership companies, but nearly all work the same. If this information is not pertinent to your ownership, you can visit my website at www.mytimeshareinsider.com and/or subscribe to my blog so I can personally assist you with your program. If I am inexperienced with your resort, my company is more than happy to research it and get the information you need.

There are two important questions to take into consideration when dealing with any type of company: how do they make money, and which laws and rules must they follow? If you know the answers to these questions, you will give yourself a tremendous advantage over every other person who does not think outside the box. Utilizing your ownership to increase the money-making opportunities for your developer will allow you more time with your ownership as well as a lot more value.

First, we will discuss how to get prime time weeks in prime time locations at fantastic properties. I do not know how many times I have heard, "I can never get into New York, Hawaii, Alaska, San Francisco, Tahiti, China, Japan or numerous other places of high caliber." The reason you cannot get in is obvious: everyone wants to go there, and there are very few rooms.

If you would like a prime week inside your resort group, there are not a lot of tricks besides booking early if you are not going to trade. My advice to you is this:

Deeded week owners

Find out the business hours for the reservations department as well as which time zone they are located in. Ask if there is any special part of your membership that allows you to book out farther than standard owners. This will make a big difference. For example, if you are a Wyndham owner, you have priority at the resort where you are deeded as well as reservation assistance to book out up to three months ahead of regular owners who do not have a deed at that location.

If there are any advantages such as these, you must definitely exploit them to get what you want. In nearly all cases, just booking a couple of weeks ahead of everyone else will yield you nearly every reservation you could ever want.

If this is the case and you do have a priority booking window, make the reservation for New Years, Mardi Gras, or whatever prime location and time you want on the day that window becomes available. Book your time whether you know you are going, or even if you think you might go. Do not be afraid to make reservations even if you are not sure you are going, because you can always cancel them with no penalty in nearly all cases, as long as you do it in the right time frame.

> **Insiders Tip:** it is always best to not leave your points sitting in your account, especially if you like to travel on short notice.

If you are a standard owner who has not made the financial commitment to be in the elite memberships don't be upset. People who invest more money usually get perks that standard owners do not. Do not get bitter; just get better. In most cases, you can do the same things just by being knowledgeable and without spending the extra money.

Most deeded week resorts have standard check in and out dates, such as Friday to Friday, Saturday to Saturday, Sunday to Sunday, and so on. All you need to do is decide which dates you want to go.

Example:

You want to spend New Year's Eve in Las Vegas. The booking center is in Orlando, Florida and the hours are Monday through Friday, 8:00 a.m. to 10:00 p.m., Saturday 8:00 a.m. to 5:00 p.m., and closed on Sunday. These are Eastern Standard Times. Resort rules say you can book twelve months in advance if your stay is a full week and six months if it is less than a week.

The correct and typically only way you are going to get this reservation on a continuous basis is if you live on the West Coast and call on Monday, December 26, 2010 at 5:00 a.m. Pacific Standard Time to reserve the week of Sunday, December 25, 2011 through January 2, 2012 with a Sunday check-in. This would ensure you New Year's Eve every year. Once you have this reservation, you can always potentially change it that following Friday at 5:00 a.m. to see if you can get Friday, December 30, 2011 to January 6, 2012, if that would be more accommodating.

The main points of booking reservations at deeded week resorts are:

- Know the booking guidelines for the property or club where you own your timeshare.

- Find out the earliest day you can call to reserve the time you would like to book.

- Call five minutes before the exact time when the reservation lines open up (check to see if you can book even further ahead if you do it on-line).

- Make a reservation early enough to get the dates you want, even if you are not sure you can go. You can always cancel or change it.

- If you own a specific week, book it in the appropriate time frame allotted to ensure a confirmation.

Insider Tip: if your developer allows you to use your deeded week in smaller increments, such as two, four, or five nights at a time, make sure to get the whole week ahead of time and switch the reservation to the smaller increments later, when your preferred booking window is available. Many points developers like WorldMark and others will also do an audit of your account if you book a week and check out early. Resorts legally cannot charge twice for the same room, so if you book a week and don't stay the whole reservation, you can call the owner services or reservation department and ask them to audit your account. If they rented that room out to another owner or for a cash rental, they will refund your extra points back.

The reason to make your reservation like this is in most cases if you book a shorter reservation, you have a shorter booking window, like ten, six, or three months, for example. What typically happens if you wait for that window is that everything is booked up and you do not get the reservation. Most resort reservation systems have rules against that, but there is usually a way around everything. In most cases-not all-you can cancel reservations during the appropriate short-term booking window. Ask to speak with a manager and plead with him or her to change your seven night reservation to a shorter one using your skills of persuasion. Most developers do not want to upset owners, so if you ask nicely, more times than not you can get them to switch the reservation without losing the extra time. Therefore, if you just wanted to go to Lake Tahoe for three nights on New Year's but you had to book the whole week to get it, you can save your days or points. Some computer systems will not allow the companies to make this type of change, but it is always worth a try.

By knowing just this one trick you can get tremendous value out of your timeshare, as well as the dates you've always wanted. Even if you are not sure where you want to go in a particular year, try to get a good week reserved, just in case. Having a prime week reserved gives you the ability to trade for multiple weeks, stay at the best resorts, or rent your timeshare out for an above-average price.

The key to the game is leverage, which means having what people and companies are looking for. Everything boils down to the same thing; where is the money? If you want to use your timeshare at the good times of the year at top-notch places, you need to know how to work the game.

If you are like me, you work hard all year to provide for your family, start new businesses, take care of the house, or attend to your family business. All you want is a nice week of vacation; vacation where you do not have to wake up at dawn, listen to people complain, drive in traffic, and spend many hours at work. But when you call, they say "I'm sorry, that's all booked. You should have called two years ago or last Sunday at 9:00 a.m." I know that is not exactly what you want to hear after you spent $20,000 up front and are paying $400 to $1000 a year in maintenance fees when you have only used the property once. If this has happened to you before, you're going to be very grateful for this advice. I live in Las Vegas, so when you come see me, you will be hugging me, taking pictures, and bringing me some nice cigars.

Nearly everyone has had trouble booking a room at one time or another. If you have ever tried to book holidays at one of your resorts without a huge advance notice, you know what I am talking about. If you have ever called Resort Condominiums International (RCI) and asked if you could trade for a vacation in New York, Chicago or Hawaii, you understand.

If you ever want to stay at the best resorts in the cities you want to see at the times you want to travel, then please do the aforementioned whenever possible.

Points owners

If you own at a points resort, it works very much in a similar way to deeded weeks, except the nice part is that you can usually book your reservation beginning on any day of the week with a few exceptions. Offhand, I know Diamond Resorts points and probably Marriott points still have to check in on certain designated nights, like Friday, Saturday, and Sunday. Whatever the case is, the rules are still the same:

- **The first thing you do is decide exactly which reservation dates you want or approximately when you want to go. Book those dates at the particular resort you would like to visit.**

- **For those of you who are looking to trade your weeks for a nicer resort or somewhere your company does not have property, remember: every year, whenever possible, try to have a little game plan to make your life easy. Vacation planning is supposed to be fun, not work.**

I am lazy so I try to make my vacation planning as easy as possible. This is my plan to try to make your life easier.

The first step

Find out which one of the resorts in your resort group is the most popular five-star resort with the highest demand. In most cases, your resort developer has resorts in Hawaii, Las Vegas, New York, Myrtle Beach or Orlando. Once you know which one is the best, find out what the most popular time of the year is for that resort. This will be New Year's in most places. There are also specialty weeks like the Olympics, Daytona 500, and the Super Bowl; these are also good times to book.

At this point, you are in good shape. You know the best resort in your group and you know what the hottest week to book is.

Example: *If you own points with Wyndham or Marriott, book New Year's week at the Las Vegas Grand Desert property or the Marriott Kaanapali Ocean Club.*

The Next step

Your next step is to know what time zone the reservation center is in, as well as what time they open on the first day you can call in advance.

Example: You want December 26, 2011 through January 3, 2012 at the Grand Desert in Las Vegas. As an owner, you can book that week ten months in advance if you do not have a deed there. If you do have a deed, book the same way during the appropriate window of thirteen months or whatever your advance window allows.

You are going to make your reservation on February 26, 2011, which is a Tuesday, at 5:00 a.m. Pacific Standard Time, because the call center is in Florida. If you simply set a reminder on your phone or computer once a year, you will get the reservation you want a majority of the time. Also always make sure you book a two-bedroom over anything else.

At this point you have a great week reserved and you can get nearly anything you want for it.

> **Insider tip:** Wyndham, Starwood and a few others have relationships with RCI and Interval International (II) in which you do not need to deposit an actual week. This allows RCI and II to simply pick whatever week they want out of their inventory. This means you do not have to reserve a week to deposit in RCI or II, but all other exchange companies will require it.

Many companies say they have the best trading power with RCI or II because of the location of their resorts, but the industry changes so often that in many cases these companies can lose their exchange power. It is important to stay knowledgeable about the industry and which areas are in the highest demand year after year. If you have questions, you can always go to www.mytimeshareinsider.com. Nearly every resort you will go to will tell you they have great trading power; however, I believe that sticking with the old fashioned way that makes the exchange companies money will yield the best results. Developers are still able to charge more for holiday and prime time weeks because of the fact they still have a higher exchange value with the exchange companies. Exchange companies make money off exchanges, so the better weeks they have the more exchanges they can get, which equals more profit. That is why RCI got in trouble for having an internal rating system for their weeks that no members knew about. This is why other exchange companies, like Dial an Exchange only charge $1 to trade a prime time week in Hawaii, Las Vegas, California coast, etc.

Now that you have waited until the morning of the first day of your booking window and you have the confirmation number, you can relax. By planning this out, you have saved yourself a lot of time and aggravation, and it only took a few minutes of planning and a few minutes to book. Now you have excellent negotiating power when you are ready to book the reservation you really want.

In short, my advice is to book what you want at a precise time rather than just willy-nilly. You will save your time, money and a lot of aggravation even if you have no idea where you want to go. Once a year, just book out the best week possible.

If you want to book less than a week, please follow the same guidelines and see your success rate increase dramatically. It is never much fun when you spend all that money for no results and you still have to pay for a hotel. Even though it is tough sometimes to use a timeshare, I still prefer them over a hotel any day of the week. I just stayed at the Ritz Carlton in Lake Las Vegas and I would prefer nearly every timeshare room to that one, which cost $600 per night.

Chapter Three

How to trade your timeshare

Most timeshare owners find trades one of the most frustrating parts of ownership. In a lot of cases, people write it off forever. When you bought your timeshare, you were so excited that there were eighty-seven resorts in Hawaii and, seventy in Cabo San Lucas, Italy and everywhere else. The salesman assured you that you could go wherever you wanted when you wanted, and after you paid $20,000 you were positive that it would work.

A year or two rolls by and you forget to use the "free vacation" they gave your family for buying. No matter; you will just call up RCI and book your trip for Hawaii. I mean, it is still a year out. When you call they say, "I'm sorry, we do not have anything available at this time." Not a big deal; how about getting a week in New York City or Chicago? "We're sorry sir/ma'am, we just don't have anything available in those places, but I will put you on the waiting list and we'll contact you when we get something." So two years passes by and you have not heard anything except for a call saying that your points or time are going to expire. As frustrating as that is, you let it go and wait until next year, because surely they will have something in Cabo San Lucas. Then you call to book Cabo San Lucas, and the only thing they have is a studio or one-bedroom in San Jose Del Cabo, twenty miles from a swimmable beach, or downtown Cabo San Lucas in a three-or four-star resort when you bought a five-star resort.

A large majority of people at every resort where I have worked find these problems commonplace. I think WorldMark and Wyndham vacation resorts (Fairfield) owners have the easiest times, along with Starwood, Hilton and Marriott owners, but I haven't worked everywhere. The reason they have such an easy time trading is that RCI, has a special relationship with points programs which allow you to use any of the weeks in their system and they treat every trade as a New Year's week type of value. If you own a points' program, the exchange companies, (RCI and II) have access to your company's inventory, unlike the more traditional timeshares.

The sad part is that a majority of timeshare owners have one or two bad experiences with the exchange companies and decide never to use them again. Most timeshare owners don't know there are ten different exchange companies, and all of them have different levels of customer service and specialties. Not utilizing the exchange system is bad because it is typically the best part of your timeshare, allowing you to get ten times the value of your ownership.

Owners complain all the time about the quality of their home resorts and about the booking process. A lot of that would change if the owners were better educated. The problem is you only have about two to four hours of education when you first buy your timeshare, during which you just learn what it is about, not how to use it. Most resort companies have owner education classes as well as owner updates; unfortunately, it can be years before you can attend one. I do highly recommend that everyone attend an owner education whenever possible to learn the tricks of their specific systems. As I mentioned earlier, if I don't cover what you need for your system in this book, you can go to my website for help with any of your questions.

If you use the system the way I teach you, by next year you will be relaxing at a five star resort ranked top in the world with your spouse or family, having a great time. The goal is for you to be able to do this for a fraction of the cost while utilizing your ownership program, all without paying an exchange or maintenance fee whenever possible. You will still have to pay up front for those things, but can offset most, if not all, of the expenses you incur with your timeshare.

Timeshares, again, are not the cheapest way to vacation by any means. Where you get the value out of timeshare is by staying in rooms that are $150 to $3,000 per night for the same price you would pay at the low-cost sites. You are also not staying in hotel rooms; you are staying in condos with many benefits that allow you to save money on food and activities.

Now that you are being educated on how to use your timeshare, there is no reason why you shouldn't be taking a couple of trips a year that you will remember for the rest of your life. Your first priority on a yearly basis if you are not going to stay at a resort inside your system is to book a prime time week like we discussed in the previous chapter. A prime time week is a full week reservation at a five-star resort in a two-bedroom unit in a prime location, such as Las Vegas, Hawaii, Anaheim, New York, etc. If you are a WorldMark and soon Wyndham vacation resorts owner using RCI, they will already assume you have this week and you can disregard the first part of these instructions. If you are a Wyndham or points' club owner and you are using any company besides RCI, then these rules are still applicable.   If you are using RCI with Wyndham, then just use the confirm-first method they offer and follow the rest of the suggestions I will give.

After you have booked your week like we discussed, you have the upper hand in getting what you want when you want it. Trading is like trading baseball cards: whoever has the best card gets the most for it. No matter which exchange company you use, they all have one thing in common: they are all in business to make as much money as possible, so they give priority to owners with the ability to make them more money. When you give an exchange company a prime time week, you set off a chain reaction that makes their business model work.

Example: You give an exchange company New Year's week in Las Vegas at a five-star resort. They put that into their pool of weeks for their members to use. Usually there is a line a mile long of people wanting to go to Vegas, but there are only seventeen (give or take) resorts that are timeshare.   To give a point of reference, Hawaii is usually the second most popular destination, and it has approximately eighty timeshare resorts. Orlando is usually number three, and it has around one hundred resorts. So you have all of these people trying to get into Vegas and all they have is a few resorts, so the demand is greater than the supply. As simple economics go, the greater the demand the greater the value.

Once you have given a prime time week to an exchange company, someone else gives up a prime time week in New York to take yours, and then someone trades for that from San Diego, and then someone from Orlando, and so on and so on. This means that the one week you gave them spawns many trades for which the exchange companies make almost $200 a pop. Your one week trade spawns approximately thirty or forty trades, making the exchange companies $5,000 to $10,000 per good trade.

Conversely, if you had given them a week in Arkansas, not too many people would want to trade for that (sorry to everyone from Arkansas). The weeks the exchange companies cannot trade are then listed for sale as bonus weeks starting at $99 so they can recoup some costs.

All of these exchange companies have some sort of internal scoring system they use to rate the value of each week and assign it a point value of some kind. Some of these companies make their points known to their members, like RedWeek, and some do not. However, due to some class action lawsuits, even RCI has changed and you will start to see the point value of your week online now. The nice thing about this is after you have read this book you will know how to get maximum value out of your weeks.

Now that you know how the exchange companies work you will have the upper hand when negotiating with them. The key to the trading game is having negotiating power and knowing exactly where to go with it once you have it. As always, you do not have to do it this way, and you could potentially get what you want every time with no problem, but just in case you do not, this would be your best bet to get what you want.

There are seven major criteria to exchanging:

1. How early you deposit/request your week with the exchange companies

2. The power of the resort you are depositing as far as supply and demand

3. Which season of the year you are depositing

4. The supply and demand of the region your unit is in

5. The size of the room you deposit and its configuration.

6. The rating cards your resort has received from other exchangers

7. How far in advance you request something

Each criterion has its own separate power. I will try to cover the most important ones, as some will coincide with each other.

Try to follow these basic steps whenever you are trading:

- **Every year, book a prime time (holiday, red) week at the best resort in your system in a two-bedroom unit if possible. (You can always cancel it later if you do not use it.) Book the best blue or white season week if you do not own a red week. If you own at a point's- based club, don't let them pick your exchange week; book a week's worth of points for a prime time week as if you are going to use it yourself. (In this case, make sure it is a prime time week as far out as possible, such as twelve months or more.)**

- **Try not to travel on major holidays when possible. This way you can stay at the best resorts in large rooms with no problems. White season is the best time to go.**

- Do your best to request your room out as far as possible, ideally six to twenty-four months for the week you want. If you do not know what you want, start a search request for something you will never get. One way owners can beat the system is by requesting a hard-to-get room like the Hilton for New Year's Eve in New York or a castle in Europe or a penthouse with any major developer for a holiday. This will have your rating system in the computer as if you had done it far in advance, even when you change the location to where you want to actually go. (I will go into this later.)

- Check with at least three or four exchange companies before booking something if you have time. This means requesting something without depositing your week. If you deposit your week, you can only search with that company.

- Submit your prime time week to the exchange company as far in advance as possible, preferably nine to twenty-four months. If you are like me and want to know what you get before you give up your week, then do a Request First that far in advance (Request First/Search First means they will start a search for something before taking your week.) To get a prime time week within your resort group, you will usually need to book it out a year or more anyway. Once you have done that, immediately deposit it with your exchange company or do a Request First booking.

- Ask for as many resorts as possible when choosing an area. When you are exchanging you can choose up to almost fifty different properties at one time. You probably won't pick that many, but if you are going to Hawaii, you might want to pick six or eight places to expedite your exchange and give yourself more options.

- You can choose multiple regions when exchanging. Let's say you want to go to a beach. You might choose Cabo, Puerto Vallarta, Mazatlan, and Cancun instead of just one area of Mexico. The more options of areas you give them, the more likely you will get what you want.

- As an owner, you can choose up to a ten- week timeframe instead of a single week. Instead of just requesting Fourth of July week, you might say, "I can go any time between June 15 and August 31" if you are flexible when you travel. If you want a certain week, just ask for that, but if you are able to go any time, you will get something much faster.

- Always ask if they will give you an additional bonus week or two for your one week. Then you can use the extra week, barter it, sell it, or gift it. (This is a favorite gift for accountants and service providers.)

- Whenever possible in most areas, only ask for five-star or Gold Crown resorts first, as they are the best quality. A lot of resorts are not that great and you will be unsatisfied if you own at a nicer type of resort.

If you get this system down, you will only need to spend about three minutes a year booking a great week to trade, and then spend less than thirty minutes getting what you want on the phone or online. When trading, you can expect your confirmation in most cases within a few weeks.

I have tried to design a system that is easy to use and understand, producing high quality results with little time or planning involved. This method is also set up so you can stay at the best resorts in the world year after year. If you have ever been interested in taking your kids to a Disney resort, the Atlantis in the Bahamas, the Westin in Maui, the Four Seasons in Carlsbad, the Marriot in Vail or Lake Tahoe, the Hilton in Manhattan, Dubai, a castle in Europe, a beach in New Zealand, Yellowstone National Park, a private pool in your room in Cabo/Puerto Vallarta/ Cancun, Brazil for the Olympics or any other fantastic place, then this is the process to use.

Depending on which developer you own with, you can potentially stay at these resorts for a third of the amount of credits you would typically use. This means you can potentially triple the power of your vacations or turn your ownership into a traveling winter home that floats and flies as well. In the next chapter, I will go over the multiple options you have when exchanging your time and how to get all of your money back within a short time period.

Insider tip: You must call the reservation department for your developer to see if they have an agreement with RCI or II that allows you to do what is called an instant exchange or a flex-change with what you own. Nearly all developers have a relationship with these exchange companies that allow you to double and triple your time by traveling on shorter notice. Shorter notice is typically forty-five to sixty days before the day of check-in. Most companies such as Wyndham, Diamond Resorts, Geo Holiday and nearly all other points systems will let you travel one full week at any time of the year at any type of resort for a small amount of credits. This process allows for resorts to fill up inventory when there are last-minute cancellations. Instead of just having the resorts sit empty, they would rather have people staying there spending money at the restaurants and shops. All the exchange companies care about is their exchange fee, so they are more than willing to give up the weeks for a low amount of credits.

Short-term exchanges work by calling any time or going online with most exchange companies to find out what is available for exchange in the next forty-five to sixty days in the area you wish to go. Most major companies currently let you do this online, and if you cannot do it now, you will be able to do so shortly. If you see a resort you would like to go to available at the time when you want to go, you should book it right there and then, or at least hold it for a day. The exchange companies typically have a cancellation rate of 20 to 30 percent so their inventory changes by the hour, and even sometimes the minute. If you see a week available on instant exchange at the Manhattan Club in New York for New Year's you'd better book it and not dilly-dally around talking to different family members. Conversely, if you look online and they do not have what you want, you should keep looking online or by phone at different times over several days or weeks, along with getting on the waiting list. One minute there could be nothing and the next minute there could be a two-bedroom at the Four Seasons for Christmas week. That is how volatile the reservation system is. If you're willing to put in a little work and not give up on the system, you can get into the city you want close to the time you want. The key is to be either vigilant or flexible, and you can go to the best cities and stay in the nicest places.

> **Insiders tip:** When you are retired, this is a great technique to stay at places for long periods of time, as well as triple the time you own.

One thing I think most owners should realize is you're probably not going to be able to use your timeshare at every little place you want to go at the drop of a hat. If you are expecting to use your timeshare to go to every one of your kids basketball tournaments in every city, you will be very unhappy. Just coming to the realization that you might still have to rent a place from time to time will save you a ton of time and aggravation. There have been plenty of times for myself when I haven't been able to get in places I wanted to go, and I have had to pay cash for rooms at the same places I was trying to trade into. It's just a fact of life. The funny thing is, renting a hotel room will give you a new appreciation of your timeshare and the money you save on food alone. The reason you can stay at a lot of timeshares for cash is they are usually multipurpose and have hotel rooms as well. When you deal with timeshares, you trade the ability to book whenever you want for long term savings as well as nicer accommodations.

That said, where you get your money's worth is when you utilize the timeshare for your major vacations and at the best resorts. Now that you know the process on how to complete a regular trade, I will explain how the instant exchange works.

The best way to work the instant exchange system is to book a week at a resort far ahead of time in the area you want to go to ensure you have something. Your next step is to get your airline tickets, when applicable, and have the trip well planned out in advance.

Now you have your trip booked and you know exactly where you are going. I prefer this method if flying because it is never a sure thing that you are going to get an instant exchange where and when you want, especially in Hawaii. The last thing you probably want to do is pay for airfare one day in advance.

> **Insider tip:** After your trip is booked, you need to mark the exact day (forty-five days in RCI or sixty days in II), and from that day you can check as often as you want via internet or by calling on the phone. Internet is always great, but it seems in my experience you have a lot better luck with things when you try over the phone. I believe I am a little old fashioned this way, but things usually start out at the reservations center before they are released online.

A majority of the time you probably won't get exactly what you want on your first try, so you will probably need to call or check several times. However, because of the cancellation rates you may get a nicer resort than you booked originally for a third of the credits and a nominal exchange fee.

Some trading companies will allow you to use your points at different times, so even if you get multiple weeks, you won't have to use them all together. Even though these extra weeks cost fewer credits or are given as bonus weeks, most times there will still be some kind of fee you will have to pay when you go to use them. This is fine. I will pay $20 to $40 a night to stay at a Hilton, Marriott or Four Seasons or a nice condo any day of the week.

Due to industry improvements you can now extend your week up to three years if you cannot use it or if there is an emergency.

Insider tip: I usually get trip insurance for a variety of reasons. The most important one is that you don't want to lose the week you saved all year and already paid for the maintenance fees. Most, if not all, of the exchange companies provide or sell some type of trip insurance that will give you the option to get another week at a different time.

By this point you should understand how the trading process works and how to get the most value out of what you own. As a Vinnie Lehr certified pro, you have all the information you need to make a successful exchange no matter which developer you own with or what exchange company you decide to use.

Once you have a prime time week, it is your choice how much research you want to do on the area where you are going and to decide which exchange company will be best for you and your family. You can also choose the type of experience you would like to have. As a timeshare owner you have a multitude of choices such as cruises, houseboats, campgrounds, RV parks, homes, and cottages, adventure tours, straight condo trades, tour packages, private yacht rentals, and fractional villas. Once you have decided what type of experience you want, you need to determine the best time of year for you to go and with how many people there will be. You can also go to the Timeshare Users Group, www.tug2.net, and read the resort reviews of any timeshare resort from other owners who have stayed there. Now that you have your criteria set, it is time to decide which exchange company best fits your needs.

In the next chapter I will go into your variety of options when trading and the pros and cons of each trading company. Most owners are under the impression they are required to use RCI or II and have absolutely no idea there are options beyond what their company initially gave them. The nice part is if you don't have an RCI or II membership or you don't want to pay for one, you don't have to. Nearly all the other exchange companies have a nominal fee or provide a free membership for exchanges.

No matter which company you decide to go with, the process I have explained will work. Some of them will allow you to trade from $1 to $149 in some cases. So, sit back and relax like I will be doing at the Marriott pool in Lake Tahoe on Labor Day weekend and get ready to experience a multitude of options you probably never knew were available to you.

Summary of how to trade

Stage 1

Home resort/developer points

- Find out which resort is the most popular within your developer's system and book a prime time week there. You can call your reservations department to find out this information (usually it's Hawaii, Las Vegas, New York, Orlando, or Myrtle Beach).

- Call and ask what the most important or busiest times are at that resort. Find out the earliest you can call to book a week-long reservation (such as thirteen, twelve, or ten months in advance) as well as what time the reservations department opens (time zone as well as the days and hours of operations).

- Mark in your calendar or on your phone or computer the first day you can call. Call beginning five minutes before the exact moment the reservations department opens, or go online and book a week-long reservation in a two-bedroom unit if you have enough points.

- Get the confirmation number as if you were going to stay there yourself.

Stage 2

- Decide where you want to go and when you would like to go. Typically have two or three destinations in mind and a minimum of three or four resorts at each destination. Alternatively, have one resort or destination in mind with several different dates. Choose the method that works better for your family. The more options you have selected, the more likely you are to get something.

- If you have a membership with II or RCI, call them when you have made this decision as early as possible (eight to twelve months in advance is ideal, but not entirely necessary.) If you don't know where you want to go, start an ongoing search for something you know you won't get, like the Hilton in New York on New Year's in the penthouse.

• **Do not** deposit your week when they ask unless you are certain you will not use that week back in your system. Do a Request First or a Search First if that option is available. If you know you do not want to use that week inside your system or if you are going to lose the time, then deposit it.

• If they do not have what you want (which is what you will most likely hear on your first call), then start an ongoing search and proceed to check with the other exchange companies.

Insiders tip: Do not deposit your week or you cannot search any other companies.

Insiders tip: If you do a Request First and deposit your week at a later date without getting your week first, you will lose your trading power. So do not deposit your week until they have exactly what you want.

• Most companies have their inventory online, so check them out accordingly and call any of them if you need help.

- Once they have what you want, ask them if they will give you an extra bonus week or two since you are giving them a prime time week.

- At this point, give the reservation department the confirmation number and ask if an upgrade is available. Pay the appropriate exchange fee and upgrade fee, if applicable.

> **Insiders tip:** As often as possible, ask for a five-star or Gold Crown resort to ensure the best possible resorts.

> **Insiders tip:** Trading on short notice is extremely difficult as prime time weeks are given to the owners on the top of the waiting list. If you are a short-term planner, then make sure every year you start a search for a prime time location twenty-four to eighteen months in advance. Then when you decide to trade on short notice, you just call the exchange company and change your initial search and that will keep you at the top of the waiting list. **Do not** start a new search as you will lose your place at the top of the list.

Trading completed; enjoy your vacations.

Chapter Four

Exchange companies

In this highly competitive information age, there are more options than just RCI or II to exchange your timeshare. For nearly thirty years, RCI and II dominated the industry of brokering timeshare trades. These companies were your only choice for exchange, and your developer didn't give you many other options.

RCI started as a small business developed by a husband and wife who later divorced. After the divorce, the husband started II, which allowed trades to only four- and five-star resorts, and RCI became the biggest exchange company in the world. Due to the increasing number of timeshare owners and services, these two companies do not always cover everything you need. To fill the need where RCI and II fell short, many different boutique exchange companies launched, offering a multitude of options for owners looking for things to do with their timeshares. These companies filled the gaps II and RCI left, and chose to provide a higher level of customer service, in most cases.

These boutique exchange companies sprang up and flourished because of the frustration most people feel when trying to book an exchange through II or RCI. In many cases, owners find it difficult to get what they want when they want it. In defense of the exchange companies, a lot of people probably ask a lot of unreasonable things in unrealistic timetables, such as New Year's in New York three weeks ahead of time. But in many cases people simply would like to go *anywhere* in Hawaii at any time and they are still unable to get in. For this reason alone many people give up on the idea of trading and simply cancel their memberships, never to try again. The only option left for them is to stay in their home resort networks, which typically provide no more than a handful of places to go. Couple this with high maintenance fees and some timeshare owners are very unsatisfied. For the most part, I would probably say 70 to 80 percent of owners are satisfied, as they have realistic expectations and have learned how to work the system in their favor. The owners who are the most unhappy are the ones who do not take the time to learn how to work their programs. Instead, they try to use it a couple of times to no avail. If you couple that with a negative mindset that "This thing doesn't work," then it doesn't. As with anything in the universe, whatever we ask is what we receive.

The good news is you are doing something about it by reading this book. You will be staying at the best resorts in the world while other "smart" people who say timeshares are a rip-off and a scam are staying at some hotel room that costs $150 to $2,000 per night because it's "cheaper" than maintenance fees. You will be the one getting the last laugh when you are staying at the Westin in Maui for a free exchange and the guy on the right of you paid $10,000 for the week and the guy on the left snuck in from his hotel down the street. At that point you can simply give that little smile of self-satisfaction, knowing that you traded in there for free or very little.

Whether you rub it in their faces or not is optional. Personally, I would much rather have the knowledge than tell them all about how much money they are spending on food and rooms, while I am basking on the same beach for one quarter of the amount they paid. See, your teacher always told you reading was good for you, and now it actually pays. Money saved is money earned, as the old saying goes.

Let's go through the variety of resources you will now have available to you. The nice thing is instead of having to do all of the research yourself, I have done all of it for you.

What type of exchange are you looking for?

- Are you looking for your once-a-year big vacation for a week?

- How far in advance do you want to book?

- What size room are you looking for, and do you need airfare, car rental, etc?

- In what city are you looking, and in what country?

- Are you looking for a standard condo, cruise, house boat, all-inclusive, or tour vacation?

- How much money are you looking to spend?

- With which exchange companies do you have memberships?

- Do you have your prime time week booked and ready to trade?

- How much time do you have to book this trip?

If you just take one or two minutes to answers these questions before planning your vacation, you can save yourself a lot of time and hassle. Imagine: year after year you are staying all over the world. You are at the Marriott in Maui with a beach-front room, drinking a glass of wine in the Jacuzzi, or at the Atlantis Resort in the Bahamas on the most beautiful grounds you can imagine, swimming with the dolphins, watching the kids go around the lazy river rapids, and dining on the freshest fish, all included. Next year, you're staying at the Four Seasons in Carlsbad, California, going to a jazz festival one day and taking the kids to Lego land the next, and then off to a round of golf were they play the US Open, all for $125. One year you might decide to stay in Las Vegas at the Westgate Planet Hollywood Tower on the strip with remote control shades and; plasma screen TV's in the bathrooms, gambling and exploring all of the fabulous nightclubs, restaurants, and gaming. That winter, your family may jet off to Aspen, Lake Tahoe, Park City, or Whistler to go skiing at a ski-in, ski-out resort with a tram that goes from your resort to the top of the mountain with discounted tickets. You can enjoy your family as they ski down the mountain. Now, imagine being able to do things like this year after year with little or no time planning, not paying any maintenance fees, and paying up to 70 to 80 percent off of retail price. Best of all, it will take you hardly any time or effort on a yearly basis.

Now that you're ready to vacation, let's get your game plan together. You can also go to my website (www. mytimeshareinsider.com) to get some easy-to-download forms that will walk you through what to do step by step.

If you have been following the protocol of this book, you should already have a prime time week in your resort group booked and ready to trade. Typically, you should already have a membership with one of the major exchange companies such as II or RCI, so that is where you should try first when exchanging to avoid any additional fees and to give them the benefit of the doubt.

Contacting your primary exchange company first should yield you the best results in a large variety of occasions simply due to the sheer number of members they have. It makes sense that the larger the membership of an exchange company, the more they will have available. This means that your chances of getting something are far greater than going with a small company that only has a few thousand members. The game is to shoot for high percentage options when trading to hard-to-get destinations. Currently, the trading process is not available online with most developers; however, I believe your best bet is to call on the telephone anyway.

I am still hesitant in most cases to use RCI because of the many problems owners have faced over the last twenty years and the many class action lawsuits filed against them for inappropriate business activities. For many years, people would call up RCI and deposit their week at a five-star resort because they were told to. Then, they waited for two years before hearing anything about getting a vacation. Sure, RCI would call them back in five months saying "Great news, we just got you a week in Branson, Missouri," when the owners were looking into trading into Hawaii. This is very frustrating to someone who is trying to plan a family trip to Hawaii but doesn't know which dates to take time off or when to buy airline tickets. In many cases, people deposited their weeks and didn't hear anything back for two years, and then ended up losing their time altogether.

RCI was sued for taking weeks from people and basically assigning them an internal point value, known only to RCI, according to the location, size of the unit, and time of the year. This system actually allowed them, according to one lawsuit, to rent out weeks in high destination areas like New York and Florida for hundreds of dollars per night, and then tell the owner who traded it in that there was nothing available. Here is a link to the details of the lawsuit and what transpired: **www.rciclassactionlawsuit.com**. Furthermore, another lawsuit alleges that RCI assigned point values to certain weeks internally. In this case an owner would deposit a week from Arkansas to try to go to Hawaii, but would be superseded by someone who had deposited a better week after the fact. This was all done without the owner's knowledge. Because of this lawsuit, RCI will start issuing all weeks put in for exchange a point value and make it public. Point values for the weeks you deposit will be between five to sixty points, depending on the type of week you deposit.

With this system, no one has priority over another; it is just a matter of first come, first served and the number of points you have available. This brings a lot more transparency and fairness to the trading system so people who have invested more get what they paid for. For example, a person who bought a week in Pennsylvania for $9,000 does not have the same trading power as someone who paid $75,000 for a week at the Hilton in downtown Manhattan.

The previous rules stated that anyone with a red week two-bedroom can trade for any other red week two-bedroom, no matter what the cost disparity is. In these cases, the companies don't put the person from the Hilton in a two- or three-star resort. They will put those owners in an equal caliber resort if requested. The only problem with this system was it allowed for convoluted rules whereby RCI was somehow able to rent out these high demand weeks. Then, the people who traded weeks in were unable to get what they wanted or received a lesser caliber resort.

Don't take my word for it; you can research this online and find out the results of the lawsuit yourself.

Now that the Wyndham Corporation purchased RCI, there have been a lot of changes made and management has been restructured. Wyndham has been named as one of the most ethical companies in the country. I previously worked for two of their subsidiaries, and I believe they deserve that award. For example, WorldMark by Wyndham owners have a success rate of eighty-four percent when exchanging, and they receive their reservations within fourteen days of making the request. Seventy-four percent of those reservations are made within one day of making a request. I have worked for several different companies, and that is pretty unheard of in the industry. Since Wyndham bought RCI, I have seen a considerable difference in the amount of complaints I hear from owners regarding trading. This makes my confidence in trading through RCI and II a little higher; however, I still prefer using the San Francisco Exchange, the Timeshare Users Group, and RedWeek.

I am sorry for going on in such depth, but I believe it is important for you to know what is going on so the process I explain to you will make sense and you will understand why you must do it precisely as I have laid out here. This will ensure you get what you want a majority of the time, at the best places, thereby getting more value out of the money you paid.

Again, if you do all or most of what I have laid out in this book, you shouldn't have the cost of maintenance, you should get more than one week of vacation out of every week you own, and you should mostly be staying at five-star or Gold Crown resorts whenever you travel. If you are one of the many owners who own multiple weeks of timeshare, you will have the knowledge to get your timeshare to pay for itself as well as many of the costs associated with your vacations.

Which company do I exchange with and how do I proceed now that I have my week booked?

As I stated earlier, your first priority is typically to call your primary exchange company, RCI or II, because you are most likely already paying their membership fees and they have the largest membership bases, thereby increasing your chances. There are two methods to exchanging with all of the different exchange companies: '**Deposit First**' and '**Request/Search First**'. I have had owners have much success with both scenarios in my years of business, so you just need to decide which scenario is best for you and your family.

Deposit First

Whenever you call the exchange companies they will ask you to deposit a week. With most developers, this means giving them the confirmation number for the week you have already booked.

> **Insiders tip**: You get a higher priority for every month over six months before the check-in date of the week that you are depositing. This is because the company has a longer time to find someone to take it.

Example: You book New Year's week for 2011- 12. If you give it to the exchange company before June 2011, you will have a higher trading power than if you gave it to them in October 2011. If you give them the week in November 2010, you will greatly increase your trading power.

Request First method:

The Request First method is similar to the Deposit First method, except you don't give the company your week until they get you the week that you want. According to an II representative and everyone I have seen trade successfully, either way gives you the same trading power. The nice thing with requesting first is if you don't get what you want, you can always use your week back at your resort system instead.

> **Insiders tip:** With the Request First method, if you end up depositing your week at a later date before you get your trade, you will seriously diminish your trading power. If you and someone else have the same week and they deposit first but you request first, your trading power will be equal.

The thing that I and most of the people in the industry find is that if you have a prime time week that the exchange companies can make money off of, they will tend to find you the trade you want rather quickly. If you deposit it with them, they will call and ask you to take a lot of stuff you are not looking for. After your week has been deposited for twenty-four hours, you usually can't get it back. All the company is obligated to do is find you something within two years. For this reason I prefer the Request First method to keep my negotiating power strong. If you know you are definitely not going to be staying within your resort system or you are going to lose your time, then it is definitely wise to deposit with one of the exchange companies.

Just make sure the week you deposit with them is as far out as you can possibly book it and at the best resort and time you can get.

Attention Points Owners: Most points clubs now have special arrangements with II and RCI in which you don't have to give up a week to them before they will get you what you want, and they can pick almost any week out of your developer's inventory for their use.

In those cases all you need to do is follow the instructions from the previous chapter to request your time as far out as possible for what you want. If you don't know what you want, start a request for something you know you most likely won't get, like a penthouse at the Four Seasons for a major holiday. Or, ask the representative which is the hardest resort to trade into and request that particular one. Once you know where you want to go, change your request to where you want to go. Do not start a new search or you will lose your power. This will give you the power of requesting farther in advance but allow you to trade on short notice, such as two to six months, and actually be able to get something.

I have a lot of owners get exactly what they want when they want with II and RCI, as well as owners who never get what they want. With these exchange companies, you can typically start a search up to two years in advance for a whole week and up to ten months in advance for less than a week. Currently, both II and RCI allow you to exchange partial weeks as well as individual nights, so you can save your points when you would like to go somewhere but do not want to stay the whole week. This has revolutionized the industry and given owners a multitude of options for many different things to do on vacations, or even nightly trips. Timeshare still isn't the end-all-be-all for every trip you are going to take in your life, but it will sure save you thousands and thousands of dollars, year after year, for your major vacations and business travels.

Alternative exchange companies

Everyone's priorities in life change. You may search for choices and services that your primary exchange companies cannot offer, so many new companies have developed to meet these needs.

Many of my owners have simply written off RCI and II because of a bad experience when they tried to use them. I believe this is a mistake because of the many benefits trading can give you. It is the fastest way to recoup the money you spent in just a few short years. You already know that trading allows you to get multiple weeks out of every one week you own, as well as other benefits. Some companies even allow you to turn your points in for Disneyland vacations, sporting events, show tickets, golf packages, spa items, and on and on.

You are not going to get the best resorts every single time, and the system is not perfect, especially if you do not plan ahead. But if you accept that fact and do the following you will be very satisfied a majority of the time and get all of your initial investment back in a few short years. You will also be the envy of your friends when you get back from the best resorts with all kinds of wonderful pictures. All prices in this section were current at the time this book was printed, but are subject to change.

One of my favorite boutique sites to use and a company that I recommend to all my owners is the San Francisco Exchange. This company has been in business over fifteen years and their people specialize in trading only five-star or

Gold Crown resorts with a high level of customer service. SFX lets you trade your high-value properties for similar properties of high caliber. Getting the most value of your timeshare comes from trading into resorts that would cost two hundred dollars–plus per night if you were to pay cash. The exciting part comes when you have only paid $15,000 or $20,000 for a lifetime of vacations and you trade into a Disney resort, Westin or Four Seasons resort that would normally run you $3,000 to $12,000 for a single trip. All you paid for this was a nominal exchange fee. It doesn't take many of these trips to get your investment back.

The San Francisco Exchange

Website: www.SFX-Resorts.com

Phone: (800)-739-9969

Membership cost:

Gold–Free;

Platinum–$299 for 3 years, $125 for a year;

Platinum Reward–call for pricing

Trade fee:

$189 Domestic/International; $159 Platinum

Highlights:

- Very customer service oriented

- Proactive and will search for weeks for you

- Even if you are a Gold member and you deposit your week first, you usually get what you want

- Only 600 resorts, but they are the highest quality timeshares available

- Typically will give you an extra bonus week or two for your one week

- One of the absolute best sell-off lists in the industry

- Rent out the best resorts, usually for under $100 per night

Platinum rewards

- You have thirty-six months to use your week

- Don't pay until you confirm (that's how it should be)

- You can request up to 24 months in advance (Can you say reservations for all major events: NASCAR, Olympics, World Series, etc? Two or three of those trades could pay for your whole ownership.)

- Only $149 to trade

- You can do a Request First (allows you to check out multiple companies)

- Guest certificates are free if you want to "gift" your property (Do not tell them you are renting it out; it is against the rules and up to you if you decide to do that.)

- Upgrade your room if its available (best when done in off season)

- Buy discounted weeks at $200 off

- Trade your week for a cruise

- Tour vacations (exotic locations as well as various adventures)

- Access to all major cruise lines, no blackout dates

- Earn loyalty rewards on cruise and tour savings

- Best price guarantee

- Full service travel concierge (get help with anything you need on vacation)

- Friends or family travel benefits (get your friends great deals on vacations as well)

This list is pretty incomparable in the industry, and a lot of my owners have had great results with this company. SFX is usually the first place I look for my trades, but that's because I like to stay in nice places in my old age.

For prime time reservations, try to place your request eight to twelve months in advance. For slower periods, three to seven months is recommended, but it's not a must. The key to successful exchanging is to be *flexible*. If you don't want to be flexible, then be smart and follow these instructions.

SFX will not replace your main exchange company totally, but it is a great resource that really helps you get your money's worth. The company's platinum membership has many benefits that most companies do not offer, and the concierge service and price match are fantastic products.

RedWeek

Website: www.redweek.com

Visit their website for further contact information

Membership cost: $15

Exchange fee: $125 domestic/International

Insiders tip: As I write this book, RedWeek has contracted Dial an Exchange, another boutique exchange company that I will describe later in this chapter, to handle their trades.

RedWeek is one of my favorite sites, especially when it comes to rentals. The company's processes are very transparent and do not hide the value of your week. You can exchange your week in real time and RedWeek will assign a point value for your trade. With those points, you can trade for any resort of equal or lesser value. If you have a prime time week with a high point value you could conceivably get multiple weeks for your one.

Highlights:

- Access to all timeshare resorts worldwide- that's 5700 properties, including both RCI and II properties

- Only $125 to trade, with no international surcharge

- Only $15 membership, with access to 1.5 million users who could be potential renters

- You receive points according to the week you trade in and it's all transparent online; if you don't have enough points, you can pay cash for the difference or get points refunded for later use

- View all weeks online no matter what your trading power

- Free guest certificates (you can get a great trade and still have points leftover to give to someone as a present, and it won't cost you a thing)

- Post your timeshare for rent for $25,this fee will give you access to potential renters

- Access to Red Wishes a list of people advertising for weeks they wish to rent

- Trade directly with other owners, usually at no cost

- Use First American Title, the biggest title company in the country, to collect your rental money and send out your contract, all for a nominal fee

- Private rental agreements you can use with your renter for everyone's safety and peace of mind

RedWeek has a great organization and business model that specializes in the rental aspect of timeshare trades. If you are looking to get multiple weeks for going to Europe or renting out your timeshare, RedWeek is the first place I would go. *The company's trading process may have changed by the time you read this, as it will be handled by the next company I discuss.*

Dial an Exchange Live

Website: www.daelive.com

Phone number: (800)-468-1799

Email: info@dialanexchange.com

Membership cost: Basic- free; Gold- €33

Dial an Exchange has been around for over ten years with offices in Australia, China, India, the United States, New Zealand, Europe, South Africa, and Thailand.

This company has a great interactive website where you can book vacations in real time, as well as personal service by telephone. Dial an Exchange has great customer service and is one of the best resources to trade your unit outside of the US with low exchange membership costs. The company allows you to either Deposit First or Request First, with an extra credit if you Deposit First.

Highlights:

- No membership fee

- Low exchange fees

- Three full years in which to use your exchange credits

- Worldwide exchange destinations including the United Kingdom

- No payment until you confirm

- Transparent system, exchange availability is published live online

- Cancellation protection (system restores your credit if you cancel)

- Late booking bonus weeks at very low prices

- Friendly personal service to help you get the exchange holiday you need

- A simple holiday property exchange service that does not try and sell you anything

Dial an Exchange is a fantastic resource because it lets you view all available weeks in real time on its website. If you need to cancel your vacation, they give you three years to use it at another location. Not only can you trade with timeshares, but you can also trade for private homes, beach houses, chateaus, and more in all parts of the world.

This company is fairly new to me, but I am very impressed by its transparency, varied access to different types of properties, and ability to get exchanges done quickly. Through the company's network of properties, it offers personal service and access to managed holiday properties such as cottages, villas, condos, townhouses, and apartments. This allows you access to more places and types of vacations than you can possibly imagine. If you trade a prime time week with Dial an Exchange like I described previously, you only pay $1. The primary use of this company should be for looking for exchanges.

Timeshare Users Group

Website: www.tug2.net

Phone: (904)-298-3185 or (800)-243-1921

AOL instant messenger screen name: "TugTimeshare"

Email: tug@tug2.net

Membership cost: $15 for one year or $30 for three years

If you own a vacation ownership plan, I believe becoming a member of the Timeshares Users Group is a necessity for several reasons. TUG was formed by timeshare owners for timeshare owners. This group helps with everything from renting your timeshare, selling it, discussing issues, and trading. You can also read reviews of all resorts by actual timeshare owners. Timeshare Users Group is available to all timeshare owners worldwide.

Highlights

- Access ratings and reviews of thousands of resorts all around the world written by actual timeshare owners who have stayed at those resorts (reviews include rooms, local attractions and more)

- Online forums consist of over fifty thousand timeshare owners discussing timeshare questions with experts as well as other owners

- TUG's Timeshare Marketplace is one of the largest and most visited timeshare classified sites on the internet, with approximately five thousand ads running at any given time; all ads are open to the public and do not require membership to browse

- Post ads for free for rental, sale or exchange if you are a member

- TUG Advice is a great section for buyers and sellers just getting into timesharing; this section is written by members and experts

There are always resorts like the Atlantis in the Bahamas, Marriott, Westin, Diamond, and nearly all the top-name developer weeks available for trade at *no cost* through TUG.

One of the biggest benefits is you can place your timeshare rental ads for free and potential renters can contact you directly. This gives you an advantage by having two or three places to post your ads at little or no cost, thereby increasing your likelihood of a successful rental. Another benefit to renters is the 'Rent Wish' section, where people place ads searching for a week to rent out. If you have a resort in the location someone else is looking for, you can contact that person directly for an easy rental. There is nothing better than having a renter come to you.

Another benefit of TUG is you can get all the free advice you like regarding timeshare rental or resale. The group has all of the appropriate forms you need for free. You can use the other rentals on the site as a guide to set your price for the fair market value.

When you go to trade your prime time week, make this the second or third stop on your list and the first or second on your list for rentals.

Platinum-Interchange

Website: www.platinuminterchange.com

Phone number: (800)-854-2324 or 1(714)-779-7900 (International)

Membership cost: Free

Exchange fee: Domestic $129/ International $149

Upgrades: $97

Guest Certificates $35

Platinum Interchange is a thirty year-old company that specializes as a third party exchange company in rentals and exchanges. Owners praise PI's customer service as well as its variety of resorts. The company has over 1,200 vacation properties worldwide, and you can request your week first before depositing your week or paying a fee. One of the best parts is the rental program: as a vacation property owner, you can rent out your property for any length of time, from weeks to just a few days. Never again will you have left-over or lost points. How nice would it be if you were still able to take a vacation and have your maintenance fee paid? For a nominal $39 advertising fee, PI will assist you with renting out your unused time.

Highlights

- No membership fees or annual dues

- No fees until confirmed

- One of the lowest exchange fees in the industry

- Free Away list available online

- Two for one bonus weeks

- Easy to use online resort directory over 1,200 participating resorts

- Savings on suite rentals

- Open seven days a week by phone

- Great service and value for over thirty years

I don't recommend this company for any premium vacations because the resort quality is lower than the others mentioned. However, you certainly are able to get decent condos in a lot of different places through Platinum Interchange. The best feature of this company is that you can rent your unit out by the day with only a two day minimum.

A licensed rental coordinator handles the rental for you and can answer any questions you may have. If your time doesn't rent, PI gives you credit to use for your own vacation at a later date.

Benefits of a PI rental:

- Dedicated Tricom Realty services owner rental coordinator

- Rent out increments (two night minimum)

- If your unit doesn't rent you can use it yourself for future vacation rentals

- Listing on the Platinum Interchange website

- Listing in the Global Distribution System (GDS), which is available to thousands of travel agents worldwide

- Available to discount rental programs and publications as well as PI's database of timeshare owners

I will get more into rentals in subsequent chapters, but I think Platinum Interchange is the best option for rental for owners who do not want to do the work themselves.

Trading Places International

Website: www.tradingplaces.com

Phone: (800)-365-1048

Membership cost: Free

Exchanges: Internal-$109; Domestic-$119; International-$129

Trading places is the third-biggest timeshare exchange company, and it has been in business for over thirty years. TPI is based out of California and is known for friendly customer service as well as being one of the biggest travel agencies in California, with many satellite offices across the country that provide a "one call does it all" service. If you do not own a timeshare with one of the ten major developers (Wyndham, Marriott, Westin, Hyatt, etc.) then this is a great service for you. TPI provides all necessary services without you having to do everything yourself.

Highlights

- Understands that 80 percent of people want to trade to 20 percent of the available destinations, so the company focuses on these regions

- Trade domestically, internationally or back into your home resort

- Full service travel agency accessible through the internet or TPI's staff of professionally trained agents

- Access to resorts, hotels and private villa accommodations

- Optional membership club offering a world of travel benefits such as real value travel coupons, discounts on exchange fees, cruises, condo rentals, and preferred access to the Resorts to Points program.

- Hawaii vacationers can set up island activities by land, sea or air, including tours, luaus, golf, snorkeling trips, and helicopter rides

- Selected TPI owners have the ability to exchange their timeshare week toward cruises; work directly with TPI-certified cruise counselors who offer the best choices for your needs at the lowest unpublished rates

- Premier Account Access, which is a special vacation opportunity allowing certain timeshare owners the option of exchanging use time to resorts within trading places; other benefits of this program include bonus time, vacations, upgrades, and guest certificates

Trading Places is a reputable company with many strengths that can help timeshare owners maximize their vacations, all at one low price. Depending upon how big your developer is, your home company might have its own travel agency that allows you to book everything directly, but that usually doesn't end up being any cheaper than any site you can find online. The nice part about TPI is you can knock everything out at once.

Overall, if you do not own a timeshare or your resort doesn't offer any other travel benefits, this is a great resource to use for its customer service and multitude of options.

Hawaiian Timeshare Exchange

Website: www.htse.net

Phone: (866)-860-4873

Membership cost: $49 for one year; $125 for three years; $199 for five years

Exchange fee: $79 Internal; $99 Hawaii/US Mainland Resorts, $109 International

Upgrades: $175-studio to one bedroom or one bedroom to two bedrooms;

$275-studio to two bedrooms

HTSE is not one of the biggest exchange companies in the industry, but it is another resource if you need alternative options. This is a travel agency as well as a rental and exchange company that specializes in trades to and from Hawaii. HTSE does not have a huge membership base so it doesn't allow for a tremendous amount of options, and you have to be a paying member to view a lot of their inventory. However, if you have a timeshare with a small developer and you love to go to Hawaii, this can be a great resource for you because of the travel agency.

Highlights

- Low membership cost compared to II or RCI

- High probability of getting the week you want in Hawaii

- Full service travel agency

- Ability to upgrade rooms

- Low cost bonus weeks and great last-minute specials

- Can trade to mainland as well as international resorts

This exchange company is a great resource if you are having a problem getting into Hawaii and you really need a room there. HTSE helps owners of smaller developers or single resorts get into harder destinations, such as Hawaii. Overall, it is not my favorite exchange company, but it is decent with a great market specialization where a lot of others fall short.

You are probably a little overwhelmed by now with all of these different options so I will not review any of the other smaller companies at this time. If you would like to know about the other exchange companies not listed here, you can become a member of my website and we will discuss them in further detail. The list of exchange companies is in the order I recommend if you are unable to get anything you want from your primary exchange company.

Trading is where you typically get the most value out of your timeshare, especially if you bought a week for under $20,000 and you are able to trade into places like the Marriott, Westin, Hilton, and Four Seasons. If you are able to get multiple weeks out of one, then that is a tremendous value as well. Again, I wish you much success in your trading adventures. If I haven't covered what you need, please sign up for membership on my website for a nominal fee. You can ask unlimited questions in regards to all of this, as well as learn about all the best specials and any first hand information about what is currently going on in the timeshare industry. **

Chapter Five

Nightly reservations

"I can never get into my own resorts on the weekends, and if I wait till the booking window opens, it's already booked!"

I have been in the timeshare industry for over a decade, and this is one of the most common complaints I get from owners. It is also the one that causes the most frustration. Most of you would like to just be able to pick up the phone make a call or go online and book what you want, when you want, at the resort you like. If you have any timeshare experience, you probably realize this is unrealistic, if not impossible. Some owners have unrealistic expectations like trying to book major holidays on a short notice, but there are many times when it shouldn't be so difficult. Keep in mind, timeshare is not perfect and definitely doesn't work on every vacation you are going to take. Booking on short notice is not the best way to use timeshare, but if you do the things I teach you in this book, going on short notice will be something that is totally feasible and you will be staying at great properties.

If you are looking for Vinnie Lehr to provide you with some magical trick that will get you what you want whenever you want it, you are going to be disappointed. I can, however, at least give you a few suggestions that will help you get what you want more often. You may be overlooking one minor thing that could provide you with more access, but a lot of your success just depends on you, your travel habits, and what type of ownership you have.

Most developers have inventory that they haven't sold yet, but they are still responsible for the maintenance fees. The program for using this unsold property at most resorts is called bonus time, escape time, fun time, or some other variation. It allows you to utilize your resorts without using your points or weeks. This is similar to staying at a hotel; you simply pay a cash rate directly to the property where you are staying. This cash rate allows developers to recoup the fees they have to pay on their inventory and picks up the slack from all of the cancellations. As I mentioned earlier, timeshare resorts traditionally have a 20 to 30 percent cancellation rate. Life happens and someone might have to stay home and work, the kids might have school, a family emergency might occur, an illness, or any other number of things. Because of this cancellation rate, rental time is nearly always available, but it is on a first come, first served basis, leaving busy and last-minute travelers out of luck. One of the other drawbacks is you can only book it so many weeks or months in advance, so it is hard to plan on such short notice for your major vacations and difficult to get in for mini trips. When you first bought your timeshare, they probably said you could just buy a small package and then stay at the resorts whenever you wanted for a small nightly fee of $39+ per night. If decent hotel rooms in that area were $100 a night, that probably seemed like a heck of a deal until you actually tried it. You probably called up all excited because you were going to take your family away for the weekend just a couple hours away and you wanted to save your points or week for your big trip, but you called and they said it was all booked. No big deal; you will get a bigger or smaller room or try a different resort. Still no results. I understand your frustration, and you are not the only one who this has happened to. This happens to nearly every owner, no matter which developer you own with, but in many cases you have options. If you only vacation with a week or two notice and you like to stay on weekends and major holiday's, timeshare is probably not your best way to travel. It is possible to do it that way, but it will probably cost you a lot of time and aggravation. It wouldn't be good business if your resort always had rooms available, and your maintenance fees would be higher than they already are. One of the tradeoffs to staying in nice condos instead of hotel rooms is the lack of availability on short notice for weekends and holidays. I do have a few ideas about how to accomplish this, even though it is usually hard to do. One good site to rent out timeshare rooms on short notice is www.endless-vacation-rentals.com. These rooms are typically timeshare and are usually easier to get into if you pay cash.

Insiders tip: Book weekends and holidays even if you do not think you are going to use them. You know whether you are the type of person who likes to travel at the drop of the hat or with only one or two weeks' notice. Also, you probably know which places you are most likely to go and during which times of the year. If you are able to book nightly reservations, you are most likely a points owner and are able to book nightly stays a certain number of days in advance. Each developer is different but the same basic rules apply. You should never just have your points sitting in your account if you travel on short notice. Always have some type of reservation booked out in the system.

Example: *You like to go to Las Vegas on weekends, Anaheim with the kids on summer break, and Lake Tahoe in the winter for a yearly ski trip. Your developer allows* *you to book nightly stays up to six months out and the reservations center is on the west coast and opens at 7:00 a.m. You are allowed to cancel reservations fourteen days ahead with no cancellation fee of any kind.*

Insiders tip: Be knowledgeable on your cancellation guidelines to avoid any fees or losing any time.

This is what you do:

Every Halloween, call and book a weekend for spring break in Las Vegas.

Every Christmas, book four nights in Anaheim for the summer.

Every summer, book a weekend in the winter in Lake Tahoe.

Set a reminder in your phone, on your day planner, or men, if you're like me, tell your wives to cancel the booking during the appropriate cancellation window if you are not going to go.

I know this requires a little work and planning, but it will make your timeshare a lot less frustrating and you will be able to take more trips. You might say, "Well, I want to take a big trip and my points are tied up." All you have to do is cancel them all at once and change it to the full week you want. You might even decide you want to go a few weeks before or after a reservation you have. Most resort booking systems give you first priority if you change a reservation rather than start a new one. This system is not perfect and might not get you in every single time you want, but it will increase your chances tremendously. Subconsciously, you may end up planning your trips around these reservations.

Utilize the waiting list

You may have tried the waiting list before and did not get any results. It is definitely not one of my favorite options, but many times it is worth a try. Ask the reservations department when you call in if they have a rating system on the wait list. Some resorts can tell you if you have a **Level 1** (*great chance of getting in*), **Level 2** (*50 percent chance of getting in, so you might want to try something else*), or **Level 3** (*slight chance, but very doubtful*). Most reservations departments allow you to get on multiple waiting lists up–to eight in some cases–so you can always give that a try at multiple resorts. The waiting list is definitely not the best option for getting short term reservations as many of you pros' know, but I thought I would cover it in case there is anyone new to the industry.

Stay for free on short notice without touching your points (cleaning charge will still apply)

The timeshare industry is heavily regulated, and there are many laws the developers must follow. This leads to a situation in which there are times when you can actually stay at resorts for free. Most resorts that are in popular destinations sell out fast for holiday weeks and special events, so people must book far in advance to ensure availability. Most owners in these cases just wanted to come for specific events or holidays, such as the rodeo here in Las Vegas, the Fourth of July, or New Year's Eve. In most of these cases, the owners just wanted to book three nights, but if they had waited for the appropriate booking window, the reservation would have been gone. Instead, the owners booked the whole week just to get anything. Because of this, owners often check out early, leaving the room open for the rest of the reserved week. According to the laws in nearly every state, the resorts are not allowed to charge again for those rooms, so they usually sit empty. In these cases, the empty rooms do not show up in the reservation system online or over the phone. If you can travel on a very short notice of one to three days, these "early outs" allow you to get a room without using any of your own points, credits, or weeks.

When you go to book these early outs, you cannot call the reservation line or go online. Instead, call the resort where you want to stay directly. Whatever you do, do not ask the front desk person for this availability because they are trained to tell you they cannot make reservations and you must call the reservation line. It is most important that you speak with the manager or the assistant manager and ask that person if there are any early outs or whatever that particular resort calls these rooms. If they have rooms that people have used their credits for and then have checked out early and there are no other rooms, you should obtain access to that early out reservation. Aside from paying a cleaning fee (if applicable), you can stay in any size room for the remainder of the original owner's nights at no cost to your credits. I am not 100 percent positive that this will work at every resort, but I know many people who have used this method several times and they have stayed in everything from studios to penthouses. This especially works well on major holidays and sold out weekends for the days that follow. It is not a perfect method for those who would like more than a few days' notice, but it is something beneficial to know for times when it is applicable.

Nightly exchange through the exchange companies

The timeshare industry is evolving, and there are more and more options added to the available programs annually. One of the biggest complaints from timeshare owners regarding trading used to be the inability to utilize reservations on a nightly basis. Since this problem was commonplace throughout the industry, access to nightly stays is now available with nearly all exchange companies. The process varies from developer to developer, but all you have to do is call your reservations department and ask them how to convert your week into RCI points. Developers such as Bluegreen allow you to trade your week into RCI and then utilize their points system for nightly stays. Other companies such as Wyndham have direct access to RCI nightly and can view RCI's availability from their home websites. No matter which developer you own with, all you need to do to stay nightly on exchanges is call in and figure out the process to convert your time into nightly stays with your exchange provider. You can also visit my website at www.mytimeshareinsider.com for assistance on how to complete this process.

Most exchange companies have their own points systems, so all you need to do in most cases is book a full week like I explained in previous chapters and deposit it in one company's system. That company will issue you the appropriate number of points to use as you wish. There will be a prorated exchange fee you have to pay with this; however, it gives you access to many more resorts as well as longer booking windows. Nightly trading is still in its infancy, but I suspect it will grow in a number of resorts and with additional benefits year after year.

Hotel discounts offered by reservations

Most resort developers know it is difficult to obtain nightly reservations on short notice, so they have created affiliations to make things easier. As part of their quality customer services, many times your reservation lines will assist you to obtain rooms at hotels at prices lower than or equivalent to most online sites. This gives you the ability to simply call one number even if you can't get into your own resorts using your points.

Sometimes you can stay back at your own resorts by searching for rooms online. Developers never want to pay HOA dues on their inventory, so they utilize any means necessary to dispose of vacant rooms, including renting them out on popular travel sites. If you call your resort hotline and can't get a reservation, search online the name of that resort and you might find a site that will rent a room out to you on a cash basis. It may seem ridiculous that you can stay at your resort paying cash when you couldn't get a reservation yourself, but that is how the system works. This is why you need to know the inside tips to take advantage of every opportunity.

Exchange company websites

Visit the sites of the exchange companies mentioned in the previous chapter to view their availability for nightly rentals. It is also possible to get on the waiting lists for nightly reservations just like whole week exchanges. Many times when you call they will not have what you want so this would be your best option since they have a 20-30% cancellation rate as well.

Marketing/education packages

Sometimes there is just no way to get a reservation at the resort where you would like to go, but you are desperate for a room and just have to get there. As a timeshare salesman it pains me to tell you this, and it is something I would never personally do, but it is a viable option: nearly all developers have inventory allocated for marketing and sales. These rooms are not released into inventory, but they still exist. On nearly any given day, there is a section of rooms dedicated just to marketing, and these rooms are usually no problem at all to book. You must be willing to sit through an owner update/sales presentation. Most of the time this method can get you the room you couldn't book. You will get it at little to no charge, along with a nice gift and sometimes a great education. All you do to book one of these rooms is contact your resort's marketing department. You will be amazed how easy it is to get your booking done and how accommodating the resorts are if there is a chance you might buy something. First of all, the marketing representative trying to book the room for you makes in the neighborhood of $30 to $70 to just get the reservation booked for you at the time you want. Secondly, if there are no rooms on the property, they typically have access to nice hotel rooms in the same area that usually don't cost any extra. The vast majority of times, if the company thinks you are going to buy something, you will get a room. I am not advocating doing this, because sales are how these agents feed their families. You wouldn't appreciate going to work and not getting paid, and neither do these agents. You also never know; you could end up sitting at my table in the educational seminar and learning more in one hour than you have in many years of ownership, all at little cost to you.

Again, this is my least favorite option for people to use on a regular basis; however, it is a very effective one that will get you a reservation nearly any time you try it if your resort offers mini vacations for owners. When you contact the marketing department, ask them if they are offering mini trips to owner education meetings or updates at the resort where you would like to go.

Instant/flex changes through exchange companies

There are times when you can find absolutely nothing in your resort group at the time you would like to travel, and you only need a few days. Because of cancellations when trading, weeks of time become available on short notice, such as forty-five to sixty days. The exchange companies offer these weeks at a deep discount. You are probably thinking, "But I don't want to go a full week," and with this technique, you still won't have to. If you want to travel a few weeks out and your resort is full, but there is a week in RCI for a third of the credits, it's often better to just use that week if you are planning at least three nights. Even though your reservation is for a week, it doesn't mean you have to stay a whole week. If the reservation starts a day or two before you want to arrive, simply call the resort directly and tell them when you will be checking in. The same works when you check out. There is no day in particular to check out; it's done whatever day you decide to leave. You're probably thinking, "This is good, but there still is an exchange fee." You are right, and I will show you in subsequent chapters how to limit or eliminate fees with various different options. It might not necessarily seem the cheapest way to travel until you look up the prices for a comparable hotel in that area. In cases where you must go to a particular destination, it is definitely worth the full week when you compare it to four-or-five star hotel room prices. Many of my owners have gotten really nice places for a weekend, such as the Four Seasons in Carlsbad, on these instant exchanges. This technique can land you some great properties you didn't even know existed. You will also be staying in condos instead of hotel rooms, so there is more room and usually a kitchen, which can offset some of your costs.

Book/search for reservations at the exact time the phone center opens

At most resorts, cancellations come in throughout the day and they are not processed or put back into the reservation systems until the end of the workday. This means if you call early in the morning, the likelihood of getting what you want is greater because you will have first access to any cancellations. It is also a great idea to speak with one of the reservation operators to find out the best time to book rooms, since every developer is different. Internet booking, when available, is usually open for reservations before the phone room, so find out from your company's department what time you can book online to get cancellations when they first become available.

Make friends with the manager at your favorite resorts

Resort managers meet lots of people on a yearly basis and they usually don't remember everyone. On one of your trips, buy the manager a nice bottle of alcohol or some kind of food and you will make a friend for life. The resort managers usually get the reservations as soon as they come in, and if they don't need them, they release the inventory to the general pool. Just call the resort directly, ask for the manager who is your friend, and remind that person that you're the cookie guy, or the bottle of wine, Bailey's, cake, etc. guy. You can ask your new friend for the favor of getting you a room when you need it. This is not something you can abuse or use all of the time, but it is very effective and works on many occasions. My wife's cookies have done tremendous things for us in the past. If you give people something and they cannot return the favor immediately, they are often more than happy to return the favor when possible. Booking the hardest reservations in the world is as easy as a mouse click for the resort managers, and 99 percent of the time there is a hidden room or two at every resort.

Conclusion

I know it can seem overwhelming or like too much work, but the best things in life come with a little effort. You will not use all of these techniques all of the time, but it is good to know you have options available to you. A mechanic doesn't always use all of his tools, but it is good to have them all, anyway.

Like I said, timeshare is not perfect for every situation, but if you are a little flexible and willing to do a bit of work and planning, you can take some truly amazing vacations as well as save some serious cash.

Chapter Six

⚜

Renting out your timeshare

You will love this chapter if:

- You hate paying maintenance fees

- There are times you cannot use your timeshare

- You have always wanted to rent out your time, but don't know how

- You want to make money without much effort

- You can't sell your timeshare and it's just sitting there

- You want to make real money with vacation rentals

The number one benefit of owning a vacation ownership package is the time you spend with your family, creating life-long memories. In addition to that, there are many health and educational benefits of traveling, and most Americans should do more vacationing. Timeshare provides people with above average experiences for very little investment, comparatively. As a poor kid raised by a single mother, we did not travel much until I was eight years old. I believe your first priority is to spend time with loved ones and explore God's beautiful places. In life, however, there are many things that happen to us that are beyond our control, and in these instances we require alternative solutions. As much as we would like to travel around the world for weeks and months at a time, our finances usually dictate otherwise.

As a person involved in nearly every aspect of the timeshare industry in one way or another, I can say that renting is one of the biggest and the least understood topics. Rentals are very much a part of most vacation ownership plans and a right of all owners, similar to homeowners' rights. Timeshares can, in most cases, have all of the same rules and regulations as regular real estate. Some people buy real estate to live in, some to repair and flip, to rent out, to buy and hold, or for other purposes. The biggest commonality timeshares have with homes is your ability to rent them out to others. In the vacation ownership industry, there are many government regulations, and developers are forbidden to pitch timeshares as any type of investment. The government, for once, is right to protect consumers from buying timeshares as investments because most people will not take the time and are ill-informed to make into investments. At every resort, the sales associates are told to make you aware of rental but not to discuss it any further than that, nor give any particulars. This reasoning behind these associates not helping you is very understandable. If the salesperson who sold you your timeshare told you that booking New Year's every year you could make $3,500 a week and pay for your timeshare in a few short years, the first time this didn't work, there would be a lawsuit. There is a twofold situation here: perhaps the salesman was a little generous in the rental price, and then the owner never put the ad up. The owner calls the company complaining that the property didn't rent out and he wants his money back because the salesman lied to him. This and a few other reasons are why the resorts do not teach you how to do rentals and they themselves have rental companies that do everything for you for a 20 to 60 percent commission. The companies also don't want you to rent your unit out so you don't take clients away from the units they are going to rent. Having the developer rent your property out is a good thing if you don't care about the money or don't want to do much work. If, on the other hand, you are someone who cares about a profit and would like this thing to be financially justifiable, the rest of this chapter is for you.

As a salesman, small business owner, and investor I try to do everything to eliminate as many expenses as I can. You and your family probably need money just as much as the rest of us, so I am here to teach you how to keep more of it when it comes to your timeshare. Even though the developers won't teach you how to rent because of their own agendas, it definitely is a right you have when you own something.

Being in the business for a while has afforded me first-hand information that you can't get anywhere else. If you are like most owners you are probably wondering at least one of the following:

- Aren't I still responsible if there is damage done to the room?

- How do I get renters?

- Do I have enough to rent out?

- How do the renters check in?

- How much should I charge?

- Do I have to pay taxes on the money I make?

- Which times are the best to rent?

- Is it legal?

- How do I know if my resort will allow it?

- How do I collect the money?

- Can I rent it to friends and family?

- What happens if no one rents it?

- Can I rent out weeks through an exchange company?

- Do I need a contract?

- Should I pay one of those companies that charge an upfront fee?

- Is there anyone who will do it for me?

I know you probably have a few questions I didn't cover, and by the end of the chapter they will most likely be answered. If you require any additional information or you would like me and my company to consult with you on this, visit www. mytimeshareinsider.com and become a member; then we can assist you with your personal situation. We can also help you turn timeshare rentals into a business.

Like the resorts, I am not going to promise you that you are going to turn into Donald Trump by renting out your timeshares. However, you are probably mostly interested in covering your expenses when you can't use it. I can teach you how to make decent money with your timeshare if you are willing to do a little work. While there are some risks when renting, the benefits outweigh those in almost all cases. With a little planning and a little advice from Vinnie Lehr, you can turn your timeshares into a money-making machine. The more time or points you own, the more money you will make and the more advantage your resort will give to you as a benefit.

In my career, I have come across owners from all walks of life with ownerships ranging from a few nights every two years to people who own nearly two years of timeshares. I have even met a man who had 18 million credits. This man's only job was to sit at home and continuously run ads on Craigslist, and he was making hundreds of thousands of dollars annually while traveling for free. Now, this is an extreme case, and I am sure he had good resources when he started; however, it is something anyone can do if you follow my philosophy and instructions. Your basic understanding simply needs to be that you are going into the resort business on a small scale. The nice thing is you don't have to build a resort, hire all the people, and deal with all of the problems. Simply put, you piggyback on the resorts, which make millions and millions of dollars every year. By making a simple reservation and putting a few ads up, you can be part of a billion dollar industry. There are hundreds of millions of Americans who don't own timeshares but still travel all of the time. The only reason most people don't become successful is because when "opportunity shows up it is dressed in overalls and looks like work," according to Thomas Edison.

I apologize for the Tony Robbins moment, but I find the biggest thing that prevents people from renting their properties out successfully is their lack of confidence in themselves. Most people are too busy saying:

- What if it doesn't rent?

- It never works for me

- I don't have time

- It's not enough money

- I don't want to be responsible

- They will probably just tear up the room

- I probably won't get paid

- I won't have time for myself

- I don't know what to do

- I don't know if I can rent it out

- How do I collect the money?

Some of these are legitimate concerns, and all complaints do have some weight, but successful people focus on the upside. As a business owner, you always take the risks under consideration and just plan ahead to minimize those risks. Even the Hilton, Marriott, and Donald Trump have to worry about this stuff, but they know the upside is worth it. Continue reading and follow my plan and I shall alleviate a majority of your concerns.

Phase one: finding a location to book

Get your resort directory and find out which properties you have access to that do not require any fees from you. Typically, you want to pick a resort in an area where the hotels have a high price or the destination is extremely popular.

The best destinations are Las Vegas, Anaheim, California Coast, Whistler, New York, Hawaii, Myrtle Beach, San Francisco, South Africa, Florida, major ski areas, and the like. If you can't decide which city is best, call your reservation line and ask which one is the most popular. If you're a member of my website, my company and I can help you decide.

What you are looking for is a resort you have access to in a high destination area where there are sold-out times of the year due to special events like Mardi Gras, Daytona 500, Super-bowl, National Finals Rodeo, or the Olympics.

Example: *Owner 1 owns Wyndham Fairfield and has 500,000 credits with a deed in Daytona, Florida. This owner should:*

- *Find out what time the reservation department opens up and in what time zone*

- *Consult the club rules for the earliest time to book ahead and ask a reservation specialist which days of the week a reservation can begin (older timeshares require specific check-in days, while points owners can typically book any day of the week)*

- *Mark the first available reservation day on the calendar and book that reservation as if he or she were going to use it*

Phase one summary

- *Find the best resort you can access*

- *Know the earliest time in advance you can book a reservation*

- *Discover which day of the week you can check-in*

At the end of phase one, you should end up with something like this:

Resort_____ _Daytona_____

Booking Window_____ _13 months_

Check in Day _____ _Any_____

Hours of Operation_ _7:00 a.m. to 9:00 p.m. EST_

Dates and Name of Event_ _Feb 19 through 21, Thursday_ _through Sunday, 2012 NASCAR_

Phase two: choosing your best times and booking

Increase your chances of success by booking a major holiday or special event, which will give you your highest rental price. Most holidays are good choices, but it will serve you to Google the area to find out the busiest time of the year, as that is the hardest time to find a room.

To expedite your rental, find a few different choices at different times of the year.

Example: *You own a resort in Daytona, Florida; find the dates for the Daytona 500, Fourth of July, spring break, and New Year's.*

Example: *You own a resort in Las Vegas; get dates for New Year's, NASCAR, Fourth of July, Memorial Day, and the rodeo.*

With several dates available to you, there is always a time you can do a rental. If one doesn't work, move your reservation to the next good date and try to rent that out.

> **Insiders tip:** Always know how many days in advance you need to cancel your reservation so you do not lose your time. Mark that a day or two ahead in your calendar.

The nice thing is once you have these dates you can use the same events and holidays every year.

> **Insiders tip:** Always check the dates annually, especially for events, because dates may vary from year to year.

Pick a date at least nine months ahead of the day you are starting to book out. Try to pick an event for which the booking window hasn't opened up yet to ensure availability.

Example: *You decide to book out Las Vegas for New Year's and you can book twelve months ahead of time. The reservation center opens at 7:00 a.m. PST and you can book any day of week.*

As an owner, you call on December 26 of the current year, say 2010 at 6:59 a.m. PST, and book December 26 of the following year in a one-or two-bedroom. Get a confirmation and book it in your name as if you are going.

Follow the same process for any additional dates. The key is to pick popular dates and to make a note of the exact first day and time you can call to ensure availability.

Phase two summary:

- *Choose your best resort for rental*

- *Choose four or five dates to rent out*

- *Make reservations for the date you selected exactly the first day possible at the exact time the reservation center opens*

- *Get confirmation number and put a reservation in your name and do not tell them you are renting*

Phase three: marketing your week

The first two phases shouldn't have taken too much time—maybe an hour or two, depending upon whether or not it is your first time.

Now that you have a reservation for a prime time week in a high destination area, it's time to start marketing it for rental. **Never**, in any case, pay any companies that call you on the phone and say they will rent out your timeshare for you. In 98 percent of all cases they are scams; you will never get your money back, and you have no chance of getting your week rented. You can rent it very easily yourself. These companies have a great story-I should know, I worked for one when I was twenty-one years old, before I got into the industry. It took me about three months before I realized everything I was saying was not even close to what was being done behind the scenes. Once I realized what was being done, I left and have since made it my mission to see that no other owner gets taken advantage of again. These companies have many different scenarios they try to sell you on, but don't fall for them. Timeshare resale scams are the number one consumer complaint in the country. I have seen many owners pay these types of companies with no results. You can definitely rent your timeshare out on your own if you just follow this process. I have also included some legitimate companies where you can go for help.

One of your first priorities is to decide if you are renting out one week or multiple weeks. This will determine which method of marketing is the best for you. If you are going to rent out multiple weeks, it is usually best to rent them at the same time. That way, you only have to pay for one ad. After the first few times you will become a pro, and every year it will get easier and easier.

I haven't been able to check out every site in the world, so if you find any I haven't mentioned, please let me know. Here are the best places I found so far to rent out timeshares with the best results at the lowest prices.

Best timeshare rental websites

www.flipkey.com

www.homeaway.com (iPhone app)

www.craigslist.com (iPhone app)

www.redweek.com

www.platinuminterchange.com

www.vrbo.com

www.extraholidays.com

www.tug2.net

www.vacationtimesharerentals.com

www.sellmytimesharenow.com

www.timesharetoday.com

This is a small list to get you started, and I stopped here because I don't want to overwhelm you. Quite frankly, there are hundreds of sites to help you rent out your timeshare; however, just two or three good ones are all you really need. If you have a good week, you shouldn't have a problem getting it rented if you follow these simple steps.

The best place to go for legitimate advice and to speak with other timeshare owners is the Timeshare Users Group. This is an advocacy group run by timeshare owners where you can chat online as well as ask questions of other timeshare owners. Another great resource is my website, where you can join and ask questions as much as you like pertaining to the rental aspect. RedWeek has also become an industry leader in the secondary market with a streamlined process and plenty of services and advice areas on their site.

As a landlord, I would make you pick two or three good sites from this list and just use the same ones year after year, switching only if you don't obtain results.

Example: *You have New Year's week booked in Las Vegas and it is seven months before the check-in day. Place your ad on RedWeek, Craigslist, the Timeshare Users Group, as well as Facebook. Start advertising a minimum of six months in advance, no matter where your rental is.*

Each website has its own attributes and it would take me too long to go through all of them in this book. If you require further explanation of each site, go to the sites directly and do the research yourself. To make your life easy, I have personally checked all the sites listed above and I am confident referring you to them. As with anything in life, however, I recommend you check things out for yourself. The qualifications I used for this list were based on the ease of use, cost, time spent online, and your likelihood of exposure to quality renters. You are probably very busy yourself, working, taking care of your family, and enjoying your free time. I have set up a strategy that won't take more than a couple of hours of your time annually. It takes little to no work and has very few complications.

Rental website profiles

Here are brief profiles on a few of the above-mentioned websites to help you rent out your property. All prices mentioned were current at the time of printing.

RedWeek

www.redweek.com

Membership is $15 and a rental ad is $24.99. RedWeek has been in business for nearly twenty years and has streamlined the rental process. They have a step-by-step approach to rentals with no large fees involved. Simply click on "Sell/Rent your timeshare" and follow the instructions. The site typically will already have your resort's information with pictures already listed. As an owner, you click on a few boxes such as check-in dates, cost per night, and amenities, and then your ad is complete. Your ad will stay listed for six months, and potential renters can contact you directly by email. Once you have found a renter, RedWeek also has a rental escrow service available. All you do is fill out a small form with the renter's email address, and First American Title handles the entire transaction. This is the biggest title company in the US, and it has been in business for around one hundred years. First American Title is a fortune 500 company that does everything including collecting the money from your renter. The company collects 50 percent of the rent up front, and the remaining balance sixty days before check-in. The money is released to you eleven days after check-out. The title escrow service fee is $100 to $200, paid by both parties. To get the exact details, visit the RedWeek site and be grateful for what they have done. This service makes life very easy and eliminates most liability for you. This is one of my favorite sites and great for individuals with busy schedules.

Craigslist

www.craigslist.com

As a business owner, I am always utilizing marketing techniques that cost little or no money yet produce outstanding results. In this computer age, people do nearly everything via the internet. One of the most visited sites online in the US is craigslist. If you are not familiar with this site, you soon will be, as its popularity grows year after year. Basically, it is an online garage sale or classified ad section like newspapers of old. To utilize this site, you simply set up an account with your basic information. Once you have an account, you can begin placing classified ads. You can post ads for anything from getting a job to personal ads to selling your home stereo. The number of visitors to this site is extraordinary, and the people who use it are looking for good deals.

When renting your timeshare, place your ads under the vacation rentals section. Once you click on that section you will see a list of hundreds of ads posted by people doing the same thing with their properties. A great strategy is to spend some time browsing the ads on the page to see what everyone else's ads looks like as well as what other owners are charging. It is important to not charge too much or too little. Try to stick with a reasonable price of $125 to $400 per night (more for major holidays and high-end resorts) depending on the size of the room, the type of resort and the area. Always put your ad up on the craigslist site for the city where the property you are renting out is located. If you are renting out Lake Tahoe for New Year's, pick Craigslist Lake Tahoe/Reno. To put your ad online, simply click on "post" in the top right-hand corner of the page. The site will walk you through each step of placing your ad. The directions are pretty simple to follow, but if you need help, become a member of www.mytimeshareinsider.com and we can assist you.

Insiders tip: Put a good title on your ad to catch potential renters' eyes.

Example:

Go to www.craigslits.com

City: (click wherever your condo is)

Under "**housing**": Go to "vacation rentals"

Research: Prices for similar time in other ads

Click on "post" in the top right corner

Enter: *your email and password*

Click on: *" I am offering housing"*

Under category: *" Vacation Rentals"*

Rent: *enter your nightly rate*

Posting title: *Las Vegas New Year's!*

Location: *Las Vegas*

Reply to: *Your email*

In the description area: give detailed descriptions of the resort and amenities, as well as a link to the property's official website.

Add/Edit images: find pictures of the resort you have and upload these photos here.

Press Continue: and you are done.

Warning: It is only legal to upload photos if they are not copyright protected. I recommend just posting pictures you have taken of the resort, or just put a link to the website in the description area so renters can go see for themselves. Don't worry if you can't figure it out; a lack of pictures will not mean you can't find a renter.

Insiders tip: Update your ads every few days to keep them at the top of the list.

As far as allowing potential renters to contact you, your options are to display your email, hide your email and use the one craigslist provides, or put your cell phone number in your ad. This way, you get the renters when they are ready to make reservations. Because of the number of visitors to Craigslist, this is one of my favorite options for renting out property.

When someone has contacted you and you have agreed upon a price, you can have the renters pay you through PayPal or First American Title. For First American Title, go to www.redweek.com and look under the rental section. We will discuss accepting payments and renters' insurance in Phase Four.

Flipkey

www.flipkey.com

If you are an owner with multiple properties or weeks, this is a great site with tons of monthly traffic. You pay a fee of $20 to $30 a month, depending on your length of agreement. Flipkey allows you unlimited photos and access to 25 million visitors monthly. I would only use this site if you have a minimum of three weeks to rent out. Their average property listing receives more than 75 inquires annually.

Platinum Interchange

www.platinuminterchange.com

This is another great site with the added bonus of a personal owner rental coordinator who is there with you every step of the way. The services are handled by Tricom Reality Service, a licensed real estate company in California. Once you have a booking of either a whole week or mini stay of at least two days, you can advertise it for one year for a $37 non-refundable fee. It not only goes on the website, but is also listed in the Global Distribution System, which is available to any of the thousands of subscribed travel agents worldwide. While there is never any guarantee of a rental, this company provides an outstanding service. The nice thing about Platinum Interchange is you cancel the reservation within fourteen days and use that time for vacations for yourself if your time doesn't rent out. A rental coordinator can automatically deposit the time for future use, without requiring that you do anything. Platinum Interchange's program is outstanding and it ensures you never lose the value of your time.

Vacation Timeshare and Rentals

www.vacationtimesharerentals.com

Vacation Timeshare and Rentals has three options on listing timeshare rentals:

Standard Listing: this is a free listing and no credit card information is required.

Featured Listing: option two costs $19.99 per month, $84.00 per year, or $149.99 lifetime ad

Featured Listing: option three costs 19 percent of the total rental price you agreed on, this is the guaranteed lowest commission on the internet.

This site has 15,000 visitors daily and is mentioned in high profile places such as the *New York Times* and *O, the Oprah Magazine*. The best part is buyers and renters are not required to register in order to contact you. This company's rental program is extraordinary, with no upfront fees, free listings, low-cost ads, and simple commission-based rentals. When renting your timeshare, it is important to list with a company that has low or no fees and high visibility online. If you go to the Goggle ratings system, you will see that this company lands very high. Vacation Timeshare and Rentals also offers a free e-book that discusses all aspects of renting and selling as well as how to collect your money. One of the company's best features is its market evaluation service for renting and selling. You can submit your timeshare and receive three comparisons of similar properties with the average asking price. For those of you who don't know how much to charge, this can be a great benefit if you don't want to do any research. The e-book has great tips in it regarding the types of information and selling features you should put in your ads to get the best results.

Overall, this is one of the best sites for rentals.

> **Insiders tip:** There is a lot of competition in certain markets. To get the most of your rental, I advise only renting out for major events and holidays, not just any old time.

> **Insiders tip:** Price your rental reasonably, meaning not the highest; try to be equal to or less than the lowest if you are willing to accept that amount.

Phase three summary:

The basic idea I would like you to understand when marketing your timeshare for rent is never, never, never pay an upfront fee. As a renter, pick one to three of the aforementioned websites and utilize them according to their instructions. Most of them have individuals there you can speak with to assist you with any questions. You also can become a member of my site and we can keep you up to date with any new companies or strategies.

Phase four: Rental contracts and collecting your rental payments

It should only take an hour or two to accomplish the first few phases of timeshare rental if this is your first time. Once you know which resort is the best for you and the best dates for rentals, you shouldn't have to spend much time on the process. Doing the same thing every year will allow you repeat business and an easy-to-accomplish routine that will make you steady money year after year.

One of the most frequently asked questions is how to collect the money once the time is rented. The best method for collecting your rental money is a personal choice, and I am just here to give you some advice. Here are the options when collecting rent payments:

- Check/Cashier's Check

- PayPal

- First American Title

- Escrow Company

- Cash

The best practice is to get a 50 percent nonrefundable deposit up front and the remaining balance due sixty days before check-in. If the renters cancel before then, you have in the contract that they lose their 50 percent deposit and you still have time to get your points or week back.

Google "Timeshare rental agreement" and a list of ten resources for contracts, most at no cost, will come up in your browser. Simply print these forms, insert your terms, and send them off to your renter. It is better to get your contract forms ahead of time so when you find a renter you can get the contract to them immediately. Here are a few places to get a timeshare rental agreements:

www.tstoday.com

www.tug2.net

www.redweek.com

www.vacationtimesharerentals.com

www.realestate.findlaw.com

www.lawdepot.com

You can also write one up yourself per the terms you discuss with your renter. Whatever your agreement is, it's wise to get the total rental amount in escrow or in your hands a minimum of sixty days before check-in.

Check/cashier's check

If you decide to rent your timeshare out, you can always have the renter send you a check. Make sure the check is made to your company's name (which we will discuss in the next chapter) or your own name. Give yourself plenty of time before the check-in date for the check to clear.

You can also accept checks through PayPal and get an automatic deduction like a debit card.

Cost to you: Typically $0 (PayPal: around 3 percent of the transaction price)

Cash

What can I say? Cash is king, but in this day and age there are counterfeit bills. If you are accepting cash from friends or anyone else, just make sure you get it before the last day you can cancel the reservation in case they don't pay. Never take a payment of any kind after the rental. Always get paid–even by friends–with adequate leeway to get your time back if they do not pay.

Cost to you: Typically $0

PayPal

If you rent out units on craigslist, to your friends, or through any other source without an escrow company, this is your best option. It is the safest way nowadays to handle transactions online as well as with your fellow citizens. All you need to do is go online to www.paypal.com and sign up for a free account. To set up an account, all you need is your basic information and you are good to go. When someone has contacted you for a rental and you agree to a price, simply log into your PayPal account and click on "request money." Under this section, you can enter the person's email address and the amount you are charging them, and PayPal will send them a bill. They can pay the bill with any major credit card, and the money is deposited into your online PayPal account. Once the money is in there, PayPal will deduct their fee of around two to three percent and then you have access to the money. You can move this money into your regular account whenever you like. This is one of my favorite ways to collect money from individuals.

Cost to you: Typically 2 to 3 percent of the transaction price

Escrow companies

The safest way to handle payments for both parties involved is to use an escrow company. The companies previously mentioned will allow you to follow the terms of an agreement and protect both parties involved. Both parties agree to the terms of the contract, which includes a description of merchandise, sale price, inspection time, and confirmation information. The buyer then submits the payment, which the escrow company verifies. The property owner then ships out the confirmation number with the renter's name on it. The renter utilizes the reservation, and then the escrow company pays the property owners, less the company's small fee.

Example:

With RedWeek's escrow service, the owner and the renter come to an agreement on a rental price and the use of First American Title Vacation Rental Escrow Services. The process then happens like this:

- *The owner completes the online rental agreement and escrow instructions,*

- *The renter receives an email from First American Title (FAT) with a link to the agreement started by the owner*

- *The renter reviews and completes the application information and submits it to FAT*

- *FAT contacts both parties to collect a nonrefundable escrow fee from each; the renter also pays 50 percent of the rental fee as a deposit if more than sixty days remain before check-in or 100 percent of the rental fee if there are fewer than sixty days prior to start of vacation*

- *The renter makes a final 50 percent payment to FAT if not paid in full upon the opening of the escrow account*

- *FAT sends a check to the owner approximately eleven days after the last day of the rental period, provided there are no material disputes filed by the renter*

The nice thing about this is you can handle everything by phone or online, making your life very easy and making your transactions very secure. Another resource you can utilize is www.escrow.com.

Phase five: sending the confirmation number or letter

Once you have a renter, and if you didn't use First American Title, it is time to change the name on the reservation. Simply call your reservation center, tell the person there you have a guest who is checking in for those dates, and give them the appropriate name. The reservations center will email or mail you a new confirmation number (and charge you any guest usage fees, if applicable). When you change the name on the reservation, it is not necessary to mention you have rented it, nor is it any of the company's business, because you own that time. Don't break any laws, though–some resorts do not allow renting, but you would know that from the time of purchase when they went over the rules. Also, RCI or any of the other exchange companies will revoke your membership if you are caught renting out weeks that are exchanged. If you rent out an exchanged week to a friend, I believe they would be okay with that, but you would have to ask them.

Once the reservation is sent over to the renter, that person can call the resort and confirm the reservation is in good standing. It is also okay to send the renter the confirmation letter before you are paid to prove you are real, just as long as you have enough time to cancel for non-payment. As an owner, you can call in and change the reservation at any time.

Renters' insurance

If you are not using an escrow company or a contract, it is a good idea to get a small rental insurance policy. The site I recommend is www.dpscondos.com, if you decide to do this. The cost is $69. Most of vacation rental websites have some sort of policy to protect you, or it's written in the contract that your liability is waived for damages. Diverse Protection Services has a special policy for timeshare owners for very little cost, comparatively. I highly recommend using them for total piece of mind. Their policy will cover your timeshare for four months and up to $3,000 in damages.

Your finished

I know this seems like a lot of information and may appear to be overwhelming, but once you do it once or twice it will be very easy and will not take you very long at all. The money you can make on a yearly basis is definitely worth the effort. I have also simplified the process on the subsequent pages, and as always, I can personally assist members of my website with any of these action steps or give any advice you may need.

Timeshare rentals for dummies (me)

Simplified

Step 1: Book a prime time week at your resort

Step 2: Advertise it six months in advance

Step 3: Get paid and send out the confirmation

Step 4: Spend the money!

This is my wife's idea of simple, so this page is for her.

Chapter summary

- Find out the best resort you have access to and the best dates to stay in that city

- Book it exactly the first day it is available for you when reservations open up

- Keep the confirmation page

- Find two or three companies where you can list your rental that are easy for you to use

- List your unit for rent starting at least six months in advance

- Once renter has contacted you, send out the contract or escrow instructions

- Collect the money

- Send out the confirmation number to your renter for them to verify

Remember, you can always go to www.mytimeshareinsider. com for any type of assistance. I also offer a rental guidebook that will help walk you through this process step by step and keep you organized with all your resources in one place.

Chapter Seven

How to offset your maintenance fees

In most people's opinions, staying in condos is way better than hotel rooms even after paying the maintenance fees. However, in this day and age, with the internet and the hundreds of travel websites that offer very low prices on four-and five-star rooms, you may question the savings of timeshare. Since maintenance fees seem to rise year after year, sometimes even doubling and tripling, it is almost a necessity to have ways to offset them.

You are always going to have to pay your regular schedule of fees to the developer, but here are some easy methods you can use to get your money back:

- Utilizing the kitchen

- Trading to five-star resorts

- Tax deductions through your business

- Using your tax refund from your interest

- Renting out part of your time

- Donating to a charity

- Bringing friends and family

- Bartering for goods and services

None of these solutions is perfect, and you might not want to do any of them, but they are things I and other owners do in combination to eliminate or offset as many fees as possible. Even if you can afford the maintenance fees, it would be extra money in your pocket to eliminate some of these costs.

Utilitizing the kitchen

If you are a single person staying in a one or two-bedroom condo, not eating out on your vacation is not going to lower your fees; however, if you are a family or group of three or more, this will definitely help to even out your costs. If you can simply eat at least one meal in a day and have snacks and drinks in the condo, you can typically save the equivalent of 30 to 50 percent of your maintenance fees on food costs alone. If you price out food cost for vacation areas, this remains true in nearly every major destination. With nearly every resort group and grocery store in the country offering a delivery service, there is no excuse to not get some groceries. Some people say, "Well, I like to pick out my stuff while I am there." This is reasonable, but nowadays shopping online is just like being there in person. If you are an alcohol drinker, this will save you a ton of money, especially since drinks at most clubs, bars, restaurants are $8 to $25 apiece. Nearly every buffet is around $20 to $40 per person, and with inflation, meal and food prices will continue to climb. This technique most likely will not cover your entire maintenance cost, but it can sure take a big dent out of it, year after year. My accountant has purchased a timeshare for this reason alone.

Maintenance savings: 10 to 60 percent

Trading to five-star resorts

If you bought a timeshare that was not a five-star or you paid less than $25,000 for your week, trading into five-star resorts will definitely get all of your money back. As we have discussed earlier, trading is my favorite way to get value out of my timeshare. Some of you may say you don't care about staying in a "fancy" room because you are not going to be in it anyway. If that is what you're saying, you probably never have stayed at a "fancy" resort and you don't know what you're missing. If you choose not to trade to the five-star resorts, that's okay too; it's your decision. After growing up poor and having never been on more than two or three vacations in my life and definitely not staying in any "fancy" resorts (unless you consider the Best Western fancy), I can tell you it's definitely worth it even if you are just going to sleep there. Even renting five-star timeshares such as the Westin, Marriot, Hilton, St. Regis, or Four Seasons off of Craigslist from an owner will cost you over $1,200 in most cases. By staying in resorts that cost thousands and thousands of dollars per week, the maintenance cost is definitely negligible. If you are staying at the Disney in Hawaii on an exchange, who cares about the $600 maintenance fees? Consult the chapter on trading to learn how to do this like an expert.

Maintenance savings: 60 to 500 percent

Tax deductions through a business

The way in which you bought your timeshare in most cases will not yield you any type of tax benefits. Writing off the property tax portion of your HOA's is about all the IRS will allow you to take currently, which doesn't amount to much. Most people do not have a business of their own, which is very sad considering in the 1800s nearly 97 percent of people owned their own businesses. You might be saying, "But Vinnie, I don't have a business and I am too busy with work to start an at-home business," or you just don't want your own business. If you don't care about saving thousands of dollars annually or having a method of drastically reducing your number one expense as an American, then skip this section, please.

You can start a business for doing virtually anything in this world for just a few hundred dollars in most cases. Any accountant, business coach, or success guru will tell you the only way to get ahead is to start a small business. If you have worked your job for many years, you can do consulting in your field as an in-home business, or if you own a rental property or two you can use that as a business. Every house I have owned has been put into a corporation, and I have used it as a real estate business with my timeshare as part of the business as well. You might even start your own travel business online for $200 and book all of your friends' and family's trips while writing off almost all of your travel expenses as legitimate business costs. As a fellow citizen, I am not telling you to lie or defraud the government in any way, shape, or form. I am only saying that you can use the laws that are currently in place to their full advantage. Most people think you have to own a grocery store, gas station, or law firm to be in business.   All you really need to do is anything that makes any amount of money. There are over 20 million small businesses in the US; why shouldn't you be one of them? Once your business is legally set up, you can begin taking tax deductions.

> **Insiders tip:** To set up corporations, go to www.incorporate.com. The company has been in business for over 100 years and is great for any type of industry. You can even use your timeshare as a vacation rental business; just Google "home based business travel agency" to find a nice match. This gives you a great advantage when deducting your vacation costs because the vacation property is now your business. Even if you only spend a few days a year on your business, as long as it doesn't turn into a hobby (as defined by the IRS), you can legitimately take tax deductions per IRS rules.

The best book to read for the purpose of setting up a business is called "*Lower Your Taxes*" by Sandy Botkin. He teaches you everything you need to know on how to simply and legally establish a business and audit-proof everything, saving you thousands to tens of thousands per year, depending upon how much you make. This book alone saves me over $30,000 a year that my H &R Block representative would not do, and it is all legal. It is unfortunate that most of you probably won't do this because it takes too much work and you don't want to mess with the IRS. The truth is this is all perfectly legal and would probably take you less time in a year than you spend on timeshare tours or fighting over a charge on your credit card. If you would like further explanation of how to do this better or to get any advice on what type of business to do, joining my website will give you this kind of help. I am also a fan of the *Rich Dad, Poor Dad* series. I am more than willing to get in as deep in depth as you would like for I am willing to help anyone who would like, to succeed or do better in life.

If you are willing to change your life a little with a business, here it is in summary:

- Pick a business that you are the most interested in

- Set up your business properly

- Get a good accountant

- Have a good lawyer or use *Prepaid Legal Services* (www.prepaidlegal.com)

- Try to make money with it

- Enjoy the large tax refund!

Again, this is not an option for everyone, but it is a very fantastic one if followed. It's even easier for people who already own a business.

Maintenance Savings: 70 to 350 percent

Tax refund from interest

When most of you first buy your timeshare, you finance it in one way or another, most often through the developer at high interest rates. Surprisingly, a lot of people don't know you can write off the interest. If you already have done this or are finished paying off your loan, then good for you. If you are paying on a loan and haven't received an end-of-the-year statement showing how much you have paid in interest, call your developer's finance department and have them send you one. This only works when you have a loan, but when you get your tax refund from this portion, use it to pay your maintenance fee a year ahead of time.

By then, you should have one of the other techniques established and will be offsetting the cost in other ways.

Maintenance savings: 30 to 130 percent

Renting out part of your time

If you don't care about maintenance fees and consider it as part of the cost of timeshare, then you don't need to do anything to offset them. However, if you like to keep as much of your cash as you can, then taking a part of your time every year and renting it out is a great way to recoup some cost. I personally believe you should always own a little more time than you need in order to cover your annual cost, but the decision is ultimately yours. I discussed renting in the previous chapter, so utilize the same techniques even if you are only doing a few days of rentals. Renting to your family, friends and Facebook friends is a great resource for finding people you can trust quickly and easily. As I said before, you are not going to make a ton of money, but if you rent out a few nights a year and eat in one meal a day on vacation, you will offset virtually all of your maintenance costs.

Maintenance Savings: 10 to 90 percent

Donating time to a charity

Many people use this tip, but it lives in the gray area of tax law, so utilize at your own risk and be mindful of the law. Check with your accountant or tax professional to ensure he or she is willing to take the deduction, because every person is different. It is definitely a 100 percent tax deduction for donating your whole timeshare, but donating just one week in a year is not tax deductible.

The only way to legally deduct the week is to have your church raffle if off, or have a charity sell it, and then give you a receipt for the cash value. If you are to get any donation write-off for donating your week to a charity like Vacations for Veterans, you need to get a receipt for the cash value, not for a week of vacation. Again, this is a gray area of taxation and best left as a decision for you and your accountant. You can also Google "donate your timeshare week to charity" to find out what hundreds of other people do to stay within the limits of the law. It is a deduction owners have told me they have taken and it has worked perfectly fine for years.

Maintenance savings: 30 to 120 percent

Bringing friends and family on vacations

Another option that can sometimes be fun (and other times not, depending upon who it is) is to bring friends or family on vacation with you. Most people go on vacation to spend time with friends and family, and having them chip in is a great way to recoup some of your costs. A lot of my owners say, "We don't like to charge our friends or family," and I can definitely appreciate that. It is always your choice to charge them or not; this is just a suggestion. Many people realize their friends and families are just getting a free ride after a while, and it gets a little tiresome in some cases. What many owners do, and what I do with my friends, is ask them to just "pitch in" a little bit. Unless your friends or family are just plain broke and you're taking them to be nice, they won't mind whatsoever. If you are taking four or five family members or two couples and they each chip in $100 or $150 for four or five nights, you just recouped $200 to $300 or more. If your maintenance is less than $1,000 per year, you just got 20 to 50 percent of your fees covered and you probably didn't even use all of your time, especially if you own points. The best part is you probably saved your friends or family hundreds to possibly thousands of dollars because they did not have to rent their own rooms. Imagine all the additional money you will save from barbequing or cooking in the room as opposed to going out to dinner.

This is one of my favorite options for covering fees if you have people you enjoy being with who aren't afraid to chip in. You can also say to your friends, "If you cover the airfare or gas, we will pay for the week in a room in Hawaii," or Mexico, the Bahamas, or some other great destination. Many people would be willing to pay for the travel if you pay for the room. It is not an option for everyone and may not be something you want to do, but it works well for many of my owners. Always use the phrases "chip in" or "pitch in" instead of "you have to pay" for the best cooperation.

Maintenance savings: 20 to 130 percent

Bartering for goods and services

Another overlooked option by many owners is their ability to trade their time to other people for goods and services they may need. You may have a time when your car breaks down or you need an expensive home repair; in many cases you can trade your timeshare to accomplish these things. I have had clients trade for everything from accounting services to home repairs and even vehicles. Some timeshare owners don't realize that others aren't as fortunate as they are and hardly ever get to go on vacation. Many people would gladly trade their skills for a week of vacation or even just a few days. There could be an awesome piece of furniture you find on Craigslist, and the owner might want to trade you for your timeshare. You never know; just always keep in mind humans survived for hundreds of thousands of years by bartering, and it is just as relevant today as it was hundreds of years ago.

Maintenance savings: 30 to 300 percent

As a timeshare owner, you may never use any of these techniques or you might use several annually; it is up to you. I just hope that I have expanded your mind a little bit and made it so you have several options to offset your costs if you're like me and don't like maintenance fees. Imagine how much more satisfied you will be sitting on the beach in Hawaii when you know you aren't even paying the maintenance and you're staying at a five-star resort.

Happy free traveling!

Chapter Eight

What to do with your timeshare when you don't want it

In life, sometimes our situations change and we no longer require certain services or possessions. One of the biggest segments of the timeshare industry is the secondary market for re-sales. This is definitely one of the hot-button issues for most owners and every developer, and it is something very few people understand. There are several reasons why you might not want your timeshare, such as illness, inability to travel, loss of income, your children have left home, infrequent use, or you just don't want it anymore. Many, if not all, owners at one time or another have thought of selling their timeshares or getting rid of them, but they had no idea how to proceed. In numerous cases, people simply continue to pay maintenance fees year after year without receiving any benefit. Many families in this economy can no longer afford the cost associated with timeshare and are looking for an exit strategy. I will do my best to give you advice, no matter what your situation is or what you are looking to get out of your ownership. Unfortunately, because I am honest, you are probably not going to like the answers that I give, but there will be a definite action plan to follow.

First of all, the reason it is difficult to sell your timeshare on the secondary market is almost no one wakes up in the morning wanting to buy a timeshare. I have been in the business for a decade and met hundreds of sales-people and thousands of owners, and I have only "heard" of a few times when someone actually wanted to buy a week. Nearly every owner from every developer simply went for a free gift and then spent countless hours with a salesperson and manager until they gave up and bought. It probably took you four or five hours to decide, and after a month it was impossible to change your mind.

Don't feel bad; you are not alone. This is the way most everyone gets involved with timeshare. The reason you can't get all of your money back out of your timeshare is almost 60 percent of the cost goes to sales and marketing. The costs of those free gifts the companies give everyone are passed on, plus every single person you talked to at the resort needs to be paid. The reason it is difficult to get your money back if you haven't owned your timeshare for over ten years is because you don't have all the necessary tools to make a sale properly. If the companies could sell timeshare in a classified ad section, they wouldn't pay salespeople–they would just place ads. Timeshares are sold by the thousands daily, but the secondary market is not as efficient as the primary sales market. Don't get me wrong, you don't need to have your own resort to sell your timeshare. You will, however, need to know your options and what you should expect to get. You should be relieved to hear that around 20 percent of timeshare sales came from the secondary market in 2010. You can definitely sell yours; you just have to do it a certain way.

Identify the following before selling:

- How much money do you honestly want for your timeshare, taking into account how much you have used it?

- How quickly do you need the money?

- Are the maintenance fees up to date?

- Is it paid off?

- Is there any type of time available?

- Do you have any friends or family to sell it to?

- Do you know how to rent it out?

Once you have answered these questions, if you are still ready to sell, let me explain your options to put you in the most advantageous position.

Options to get rid of your timeshare:

- Sell to friends and family

- Utilize a timeshare resale company

- Sell it on eBay

- Keep it and rent it out

- Donate to a charity

- Give it back to the developer

- Market it via timeshare resale websites

- Give it away to a company

- Pay to have a company take it

In this economy, there are more scams than ever, and you have to be extremely diligent when researching companies or listening to phone sales-people who promise you the world. Whatever options you decide to use, always consider renting it out while it is on the market to offset at least some of your expenses. Renting out your timeshare is not difficult at all if you do the things I have taught you in previous chapters.

Deciding on a price

You must have a realistic price in order to sell your unit. This is typically 30 to 50 percent of what you paid originally. I know this is not the answer you want to hear, but do some research and you will find the figure correct. For an easy way to find the sales prices for weeks similar to yours, simply Google the name of your resort with the word "resale" and you will find plenty of examples from tons of different websites. Figure out the lowest range of similar room types by the week number, size, amenities, and other comparable factors. Once you have come to the realization that you will not make a profit, you can put a game plan together to get something out of your timeshare. Once you have your units priced on the lower end of the scale, decide which option is best for you. If you would like professional help, visit www.vacationtimesharerentals.com for a $20 to $30 property evaluation, which will give you a realistic price with real comparisons. As always, you can call my company and we can help you as well. Once you know what to expect and how much you can reasonably receive for your timeshare, utilize one of the following options.

Sell to friends and family

Sometimes the easiest way to get rid of your timeshare is to have friends or family buy it off of you. In my experience, people who have sold timeshares this way have averaged the highest resale price. Many times, people have noticed you taking all of these fabulous trips, but for whatever reason they did not buy one for themselves and they are willing to offer you a reasonable amount. They know how much you really paid and are usually willing to buy it just to help you out. Some of your other friends probably also own their own programs at the same place and they definitely know how good of a deal it is. This type of deal usually ends up benefiting both parties involved tremendously. I will explain later how to do the paperwork and accept payment. Marketing to friends and family is not that hard because you already know who's in a financial position to buy, so ask the appropriate people directly. You can also send out a mass email to everyone in your address book, call them all, or release a few posts on Facebook or Twitter.

Utilize a timeshare resale company

I debated in my head for a long time about this section and its vastness, with the tens of thousands–if not hundreds of thousands–of people who have been through it. Currently, timeshare resale firms are the number one consumer complaint in the country. Nearly everyone who has paid one or more of these of companies has never gotten a return on their money or their initial marketing money returned. I could probably write an entire book just on the resale industry, but I don't think that is necessary or very productive. What I would like to do is give you a set of guidelines to follow if you choose this route. I know I said it earlier, but never, never, never, *never* pay an upfront fee of more than $70, no matter what kind of story they tell you. I have only ever heard of a small number of cases that led to a successful sale. Sure, some people get lucky every now and again, but they are very few and far between. It is possible to sell your timeshare with a resale company, and here are some of the basic timelines in terms of how fast you can sell your units.

Pricing: time vs. revenue with a resale company

According to one resale website's e-book, their statistics indicate that the lower the price, the faster the sale. The key question is this: *How quickly do you need the cash from this sale?* Time will dictate the sales price. If you're patient, follow these guidelines of marketing, and are active with your ads, your sales price will be higher. If there are time constraints regarding selling your property, such as getting money for maintenance fees before they are due or some other need for these funds, you can plan on getting smaller offers, but faster. There are many time figures thrown around online, and I don't think any of them are close to right. Here is one chart I found that seems reasonable if you market the way I am telling you.

This chart is equal to the percentage of discount you give off of the retail price.

$12,000 Retail Resort Price	Estimated Sale Time
$5,000-$6,000 (50-60% off)	4 -13 months
$4,000-$5,000 (60-70% off)	2-6 months
$2,000-$4,000 (70-80% off)	1-3 months

There is definitely no good answer or actual research on this, but it gives you an idea of how price affects the length of time it takes to sell. If it is not imperative to get money immediately, renting it out a few times will often lead to greater income than a sale. Nevertheless, if you are looking for a company to resell your timeshare for you, here is a list from the Timeshare Users Group of companies that have the most positive reviews.

Resale company sites

www.ads.tug2.net

www.redweek.com

www.myresortnetwork.com

www.ebay.com

www.craigslist.com

www.transactionrealty.com

www.tstoday.com

www.holidaygroup.com

www.atimeshare.com

www.sellingtimeshares.net

www.ownertrades.com

www.secondmarkettimeshares.com

www.timesharing2000.com

www.timesharehelp.net

www.timeshareresalpros.com

www.resort-property.com

www.bidshares.com

Here are some other sites from the Timeshare Users Group that are frequently mentioned as places to list or rent:

www.vacationtimesharerentals.com

www.cyberrentals.com

www.homeaway.com

www.vrbo.com

www.greatrentals.com

www.wasi.com

www.condoworldonline.com

www.consodsoftworld.com

www.choice1.com

www.skyauction.com

www.timesharegateway.com

www.timesharetogo.com

Some of the sites mentioned above may have an upfront fee. Unless it is under $70, **do not pay it!** Like I said, there is a lot to reselling a timeshare and thousands of options. I have called all of the "number one" resale companies listed online and they all sound great, but stay strong and do not pay.

One great thing that has come about because of all the consumer complaints is the Licensed Timeshare

Resale Brokers Association. If you want help finding a resale company that won't charge an upfront fee and is honest and approved by state governments, then go to www.LTRBA.com. They have actual real estate brokers who will assist you with the total process. Another useful site, and one of my personal favorites, is www.vacationtimesharerentals.com, where the company will sell your timeshare for a 10 percent commission.

Again, it is a very tough process to research all of these companies and get honest answers, so follow the advice to never pay an upfront fee unless it is under $70 and use only the companies mentioned in this chapter. If you are overwhelmed, just use one of the two companies I last mentioned or go to my website for advice.

Selling on eBay

If you are simply looking to get rid of your property for very little money, then consider eBay first. On the other hand, if you are looking to get more than ten or fifteen cents on the dollar, then don't sell it there. In most cases, eBay will allow you to get a very fast sale, but the units do not sell for much. EBay is one of the largest websites in the world and is one of the first places many people look before buying something. Using the site will put your ad up in front of thousands of potential buyers. The only bad thing is the people who are buying there are bargain hunters looking to pay pennies on the dollar. So yes, there are many potential buyers, but don't expect to get much for your week. It is not wise to use eBay unless you are just trying to get rid of your ownership and relieve yourself of the fees but you still want a little something for your time. It's not that difficult to sell an item on eBay; just go to the "sell" section on the website and follow the instructions. To get a good idea of the going rate for a unit similar to yours, just go on the site as a buyer first and check out the other prices at your resort. If you want a fast sale, stay towards the lower end of pricing.

There are complete buying procedures on the website that allow buyers to pay you with any major credit card. I believe they also have an escrow or title company to assist you with the paperwork. You can also use any of the companies I will discuss later, as well. As always, if you become a member of my site I will be able to assist you with this process, which can be difficult if you are not computer literate. Either that or ask any of your children or grandchildren to help you; it will probably take them no time at all.

Keep your timeshare and rent it out

As a real estate investor and someone who is lazy, I like to have my money work for me. If you feel the same, this is a great option. If one of the main reasons you want to sell is to avoid paying the maintenance fee–and the fact that it goes up every year–then this is a great option while you wait for your timeshare to sell. In a previous chapter I covered how to offset the maintenance costs, and if you pair that advice with renting it out, in many cases keeping it might not be a bad idea. Some of you may say, "I'm too busy to rent it out and I don't know what to do." Now that you have this book, half of the problem is solved. All you need is confidence in yourself that you can do it.

Most of us would work an extra hour a month to get a $1,000 to $3,000 a year raise, but we won't take around one hour a year to make this with our properties. There are millions, even hundreds of millions, of people going on vacation who don't own a timeshare, and they are all potential customers. There are around 250,000 hotel rooms in Las Vegas alone that rent out on a nightly basis. In other vacation destinations there are the same proportions of rooms to visitors. All you are trying to do is find one person to rent out one room at a sold-out event or on a major holiday. Again, nothing is guaranteed and you might not rent it, but taking calculated risk is not a bad thing, and it is the gateway to success. An extra few grand a year would make anyone smile, no matter how much they made otherwise.

The idea behind this technique is to offset your maintenance costs with any of the methods described earlier while making money off of the rental and still utilizing the benefits of ownership for your vacations. If you rented out your timeshare and used the owners' benefits you're entitled to, it could be worth keeping. There are tons of benefits to owning a timeshare, such as access to discounted sell-off weeks, last minute deals, and hotel discounts not offered to non-owners. You could conceivably rent out your timeshare and use the money earned to pay your fees and go on vacation and still have a little money left over.

The reason I propose this option even though you probably just want to get rid of your timeshare is because most people won't think of it when they are upset. Another reason is that many weeks will only bring you a few thousand dollars on the secondary market, but rentals can bring you almost the same amount year after year, forever. I have seen weeks for sale on the Timeshare Users Group for less than the rental price for similar weeks on the same site. It is your timeshare and your life, and you can do what you want, but I would seriously consider this option for a few years. Unless you are broke and can't afford the fees any longer, this is most likely your best route.

Donate your week to a charity

If you are a taxpaying citizen who makes over $45,000 a year and are looking to get rid of your timeshare, this is one of your best options. However, if you do not pay taxes or have enough deductions to zero you out, this won't work for you so just skip ahead.

Many owners who are trying to resell their timeshares have them advertised multiple places and are spending money simply trying to get a few thousand for their timeshares. The funny thing is, if you just want about $3,000 to $7,000 for your timeshare, the fastest, easiest, and best thing to do is donate it to a legal charity organization. If you Google "donate my timeshare to charity," you will find dozens of companies out there that will take your timeshare off your hands, typically within six weeks. Most of the charities will handle all of the arrangements for you, from the paperwork to getting the deed transferred over. The best part of this is the charities you can donate to are very notable and help everyone from pets to war veterans. This is definitely my personal favorite because of the giving aspect; take advantage of it before the politicians take charitable contributions away. I think it will be very difficult for them to take these deductions away, but with the government, you never know.

Once the week is donated to the charity, that organization will send you a receipt for the appraised current value or just the donation description. If you do not have a written appraisal, you may only deduct the correct marketable value of the week, according to the IRS. I am not an accountant, nor do I play one on TV, but all of this information is easily accessible via the internet. You can look up all rules and regulations for the IRS on their website (www.irs.gov). Your accountant will understand how to take charitable deductions, and he can decide whether or not to spread it over a few years or take it all at once. I believe there is a limit to how much you can donate in one year, so discuss this with your accountant before proceeding. Some CPAs might not want you to take that deduction for their own selfish reasons, so check with your CPA first before doing all of the work. CPAs don't make a percentage of what they save you, so sometimes they won't do anything they perceive as a "red" flag just to limit their own liability. This does not mean that it's not a legitimate deduction. I went to H & R Block for a couple of years, then went to a regular business CPA who went back through my H & R Block returns and got me almost $10,000 that they had missed by playing it safe. I have spent a little time explaining this in the interest of saving you trouble and giving you different angles to think about that will hopefully save you time and/or money. It would not be good if you took my advice and then your CPA was not willing to deduct it for you.

You can deduct the timeshare you donate to charity and you will get the actual cash when you file your taxes and get your return check. These days, with electronic filing you might donate the week in November and have your money by February.

Example: *You own a week at the Marriott in North Carolina. You bought it twelve years ago for $22,000. It now sells for $34,000 at the resort.*

Step 1: Google "donate my timeshare to charity." Find a charity you like, then research it and call the charity's home state's attorney general to make sure it is legitimate and donations are fully tax deductible. My company handles all of this for our members.

Step 2: Go through the process of signing your timeshare week over to the charity. This usually takes around six weeks.

Step 3: Get an appraisal on your property to make it legal for the IRS if you are audited. You can Google "timeshare appraisal" and find a company to do this for you for under $50. Note: There are now many illegitimate companies posing as appraisers that charge hundreds if not thousands of dollars. Do not pay them if it is over $50, as 99 percent of them are scams.

Step 4: Bring your receipt with the appraised value and proof you have donated your timeshare with your tax receipts for that year. Put the appraised amount in the line for your charity deductions at tax time. Again, have your CPA help you with all of this as well as deciding over how many years you want to spread the deduction.

If the retail value at the resort is $34,000 and your appraised value is $28,000, the $28,000 would be your deduction. This will equate to around $7,800 in your tax refund. This figure will vary depending on your taxable income and which tax bracket applies to you. It may vary several thousand dollars each way, depending upon those factors alone. Even though this is only thirty or forty cents on the dollar, it is generally more then you will get on the secondary market. Plus, you receive your money quickly at tax time (unless you owe the IRS money or didn't pay in enough in the first place). The average timeshare owner's household income is $80,000 to $150,000, and I am sure with the way the tax situation is going, you can use all of the deductions you can get. Again, seek professional help with this or go to my website for help, and take advantage while you still can. This one of the best ways I have heard of to get money from your timeshare once you are done with it. Imagine: you got all of those vacations, and then received several thousand dollars back, all while helping wonderful charities.

Give back to the developer

Some of you might not want to go through any of the previously mentioned techniques and would just like to get rid of your timeshare, period. If you are simply desperate to let it go and not pay another fee, contact your developer to see if the company has a first right of refusal in its contract. A few of the developers, in order to have their units retain their value against the secondary market, will buy or take your timeshare back from you. This technique is also good if you still have a loan with your developer. Don't expect to get much money from them, but you can expect a smooth transaction in most cases. Some of the homeowners associations will also take the weeks back and sell them at auction to recoup the fees. Every resort is different, so you must call yours directly to find out what your developer's policy is. Again, if you need any help, contact my offices and we will do our best to assist you.

Give it away to a company

Another option you have similar to the above is giving your timeshare away to another company aside from the developer. The only time you would conceivably pay a company up front is if they were going to take it off of your hands completely. There are a few companies I have heard of that do a good job with this by selling the weeks to companies who rent them out to corporations.

With all of these different types of companies, it is hard to figure out which ones are the best. There is no business agency to rank them, so we are stuck with the words of others. In my continuous fight to bring ethics and responsibility to the secondary market, I have done my best to diligently research companies through various channels to come up with a few that look responsible and honest. If you become a member of my site, we will constantly update our list of individuals and companies that get the highest recommendations for the best customer service. As with anything in life, don't take my word for it–do your own research when dealing with any company. I have come across three companies who will take your timeshare off of your hands and do it in a timely manner.

The three companies are:

www.timeshareout.com

www.givebacktimeshare.com

www.timesharerelief.com

If you would like to research them further, the Timeshare Users Group, state attorney general's office, and the local Better Business Bureau are the best places to go. Even though your best option is not to give it away, sometimes it just doesn't make sense to keep it. A few of these companies will charge you $2,000 or more, but they will take it off your hands completely and you may want to consider paying that fee.

Pay to have a company take it

As the timeshare industry evolves, more and more people try to make money off of unsuspecting owners. There are companies out there that have *you* pay *them* to take your timeshare for approximately $1,000 to $4,000 up front.

They do this under the guise you will be able to use all the benefits of ownership such as bonus weeks without having to pay the HOA or maintenance fees. This is similar to a Ponzi scheme, and when they stop selling new people, the whole thing crumbles. At this point, you are out a few thousand dollars and your timeshare and have no vacation plan. This is not the same scenario I described under the previous section as those companies do not offer a vacation program. It is a strict sale of your unit. I have heard of several of these companies and I know many people who worked for them. The results are always the same: the company goes out of business. It was built on lies, and members lost all of their money and their units. There are exceptions to the rule, but rules aren't made by exceptions. There may be some companies out there doing what they say, and the few I mentioned previously seem to be on the up-and-up, and they will legitimately take your timeshare. They don't allow you any perks as far as vacations go, but at least they are honest and actually take it off your hands.

My advice on paying someone to take your timeshare from you is *don't do it*. You can accomplish your plan better on your own by donating your time to a charity, then becoming a member of one of the exchange companies I mentioned and buying bonus weeks. Essentially, all these companies are doing is allowing you to buy bonus weeks from their accounts anyway.

Chapter summary

The secondary market for the timeshare industry is in great need of an overhaul, in my opinion, because it is dominated by thieves and con men. I would say 90 percent of the businesses that deal with timeshares that are not developers do not provide any type of valuable service.

Most of them are just in business to take advantage of consumers at their wits' end and who have no idea what to do.

With organizations like RedWeek, Timeshare Users Group, and the Licensed Timeshare Resale Brokers Association, maybe soon honesty and price equality will come in to the market. Since timeshare is still in early adulthood as far as industries go and most major developers are not thinking twice about it yet, there will be some time before it gets better. The more press there is on TV about these scams, however, the more quickly people will get wise and the free market will squeeze them out. Until then, at least you were smart enough to buy my book and to pass the word on. With diligent effort and more honest people entering the secondary market, in a few short years it should be under better control.

Hopefully you didn't buy the timeshare like a piece of real estate, expecting the resale to be a good investment years later. Unfortunately, many salespeople in the past portrayed timeshares as such, and the sad part is it is nowhere close to the truth. If you have owned your timeshare for fifteen years or more and have a fantastic week, you might potentially get 50 percent or more of your original price. The thing is, most people haven't owned that long and may even owe money on their timeshares. Owing money means there is nearly no way you can get rid of it until it is paid in full and you can get the deed.

Timeshare retains its value best when you use it every year for vacations and then pass it down to family members or friends. If life isn't working out perfectly for you, as it often doesn't for many, then hopefully utilizing one of the techniques I have discussed will bring you at least a respectable return on your investment.

Just remember, when trying to resell a timeshare have realistic expectations about what you are going to get (10 to 60 percent of what you paid for it) and what your bottom line is. Once you have your goal set and know the number you are shooting for, you can then decide which technique will be the easiest for you as well as yield you the best results. Be very careful when dealing with any company dealing with resale timeshares; ask lots of questions, never pay up front, and do all of the appropriate research beforehand.

God bless you on your quest to recoup your money!

Chapter Nine

How to buy timeshare

Most of you reading this book probably already own a timeshare and are looking to get more value from your investment. However, you may be new to the industry or have friends who are looking to get involved, or maybe you are interested in purchasing additional points or weeks. This information will help you either get started or continue in your vacation ownership journey.

The timeshare industry has many products and services, and deciding what you should buy or from whom can be a difficult decision. I am going to try to cover as best I can all of your different options as well as the different types of programs. Every family has unique needs, and everyone's financial situation is completely different. I have worked in the industry for ten years and I feel great about selling the product directly for the developer. In my estimation, any time you can spend quality time with your family and not be at work is worth any amount of money. There are, however, tips and tricks you can use to get better deals from the developers as well as deeper discounts buying on the secondary market. You can get huge savings buying on the secondary market, but you still need to know what you are doing first.

Things you need to consider before buying a timeshare:

- How much traveling (days per year) are you looking to do?

- Do you need airfare, car rentals, cruises, tour packages, Disney, entertainment tickets, etc.?

- Do you like to go the whole week, or do you prefer mini trips of a couple of nights?

- How much per year are you spending currently on hotels, and where will you go in the future?

- Do you already own a timeshare?

- Will your family be using the timeshare?

- Do you need to stay at nice resorts or will just any type of property be fine?

- Are you looking to rent out units to make money or turn this into a business?

Once you have asked yourself these important questions and have formulated an idea of what you are looking for, the descriptions that follow will help you. Having your criteria before beginning this process will get you what you need with the right company and save you thousands and thousands of dollars. I am going to write a second book on this subject alone, but I wanted to at least give you enough information to get started immediately. These issues are not difficult, but every program is different and most people don't know where to go to find the best deals.

Here are some of the questions I would like to answer:

- Which developer do you want to own with?

- Should you get a points or week's program?

- What size condos do you want to stay in?

- How much do you spend per year now?

- Which part of the country do you live in?

I most likely won't be able to cover every single question you have regarding purchasing, but I will give you enough information to make a good decision and let you know where to do further research.   Timeshare has around sixty plus different developers at the present time, all with different programs and business models. Some companies are good at some things and bad at others. Because of the variety of programs, it is best for you to answer the questions at the beginning of this chapter so you have an idea of what you want. Once you know what you want, the descriptions of the companies I will give should be sufficient for you to make a wise decision.   Buying from the developer versus buying on the secondary market is always a confusing topic, so I will cover that at the end of the chapter. Once you know what you want, you'll know where to go to buy it. Let's go through your options.

Which developer to choose

To see a complete list of all timeshare developers, just type "list of timeshare developers" into Google and there will be a few links. You can also go to www.sellmytimesharenow. com; under the "resources" tab, click on "timeshare resort developers" and they can give you a complete list of every company, along with a link to their websites. Then, go to the Timeshare Users Group (www.tug2.net), type in the name of the company, and see what everyone is saying about that particular developer. You can also Google the companies and see what everyone is saying online about them. Each developer has its pros and cons, so personally my advice is to stick with a brand name developer that has credibility. Big companies have the resources to add new programs and continuously add properties without any problems.

Example: *Monarch Grand Vacations has been in business for twenty years and has approximately nine properties, while WorldMark by Wyndham has been in business the same length of time and has over seventy-one properties.*

Major developers have many different options and ways to use their programs in addition to staying in condos. Larger developers usually have more cash to spend on their properties and are typically ranked higher with customer service. Buying from a small developer could benefit you if the company has a resort in a certain area where you want to travel, with weeks available at particular times. If you just have one special place you want to go to every year, then small developers are fine, but for almost everybody my advice is to buy from a brand name developer.

Here are the top major developer chains I would own myself:

Bluegreen Resorts (East Coast/Midwest)

Berkley Group (West Coast)

Diamond Resorts (Worldwide)

Disney Vacations (Mostly East Coast)

Embassy Vacation Resorts (Now Diamond, above)

Four Seasons Residence Clubs

Fairfield Resorts (Wyndham WVO/ US)

Hilton Grand Vacations Club (US)

Hyatt Vacation Club (West Coast/East Coast)

Marriott Vacation Club (US/International)

Ritz Carlton Club (West Coast/Hawaii)

Starwood Vacation Ownership (US/International)

Westgate Resorts (US)

WorldMark by Wyndham (West Coast/ East Coast)

Wyndham Vacation Ownership (US)

I don't think there are too many bad developers out there, but if you are going to make the investment, go with the best. From the brand name developers you can easily trade into any other resort out there. While some people may argue that by owning with a smaller developer they have lower maintenance or better service, I usually don't find that to be the case. Major corporations have unparalleled luxury and world class service that you just don't get all the time from small developers.

Once you have your parameters for what you are looking to buy, Google some of the resort developers I mentioned above to see which one will best suit your needs. If you find a company you think you would like to own with, rent a week at one of its resorts to try it out or go to its website and sign up to go on a free trip for attending a timeshare presentation. I will discuss a little later if you should buy a resale or from the developer. Everyone's situation is different and some people like doing business a certain way. Now that you have the developer picked out, the question is, which program is the best for you?

Points vs. Weeks

After being in the business a decade, I would have to say most definitely that the only program you should be in is points. Weeks are a thing of the past and every developer is looking at developing some sort of points program. Most Americans like the flexibility of going where they want, when they want and in whatever size room fits the situation. All of the top resort developers now have a points system, and most owners prefer the points. If you are not familiar with how points work, see the detailed description in chapter one. Points give you the ultimate flexibility as far as staying any season of the year, at any of the resorts in the group, in any size room from studios to penthouses, all without an internal or external exchange fee. For people who like to go on vacation and spend less than seven nights, most of the time, points are the only way to go. The nice thing about points is the entire resort group shares the maintenance money so there are no special assessments like when you own a deeded week. You have two options with point's developers:

1. **Points with a deed**

2. **Points of a trust**

Points with a deed means you actually have a real piece of property attached to your ownership, such as a specific unit with floating time. Points connected to a trust means you own a percentage of the trust that holds all of the resorts. You not only own one resort, you own a piece of every resort in the real estate trust.

Example: *There are some resorts, such as in the Bahamas, that are deeded properties, which means they are owned by a certain number of people. If a hurricane hits the building, each of the owners will get a special assessment cost of repairing the resort. These fees and assessments can come at the most inopportune times.*

I believe deeded fixed week timeshares and floating weeks are a thing of the past. If I were to give anyone advice, it would be to buy points and choose a developer carefully.

What size condo should you buy?

As I have said, points are the better way to go for nearly every family, but if you want to buy an inexpensive week on the resale market, then buy a two bedroom lockoff (lockoff is a two-bedroom unit that you can change to two one-bedroom units). If you buy a points program, buy enough points that you can book a two-bedroom during prime season at one of the best resorts in the group. Two-bedroom weeks will in many cases allow you to get multiple weeks out of one, as well as give you enough points or time to stay in penthouses from time to time. Two-bedroom units are also the best units to trade because you qualify for nearly every type of room. Two-bedroom lockoffs can also be turned into two one-bedroom units traded throughout the system. If you have enough points for a two-bedroom, it will help you when exchanging as well as fulfill your needs when traveling within your system.

Vinnie Lehr

How much do you spend per year?

It is a good idea to take a look at how much you are spending per year on lodging, food, and travel costs. If you already have a timeshare, look at how much additional money you are spending to determine if you need more points or time. If you are only spending $500 each year on hotels, food, airfare, cruises, and car rentals, then paying $800 to $2,000 per year in maintenance doesn't really make sense. If you are spending more than $900 a year, it would be wise to buy a vacation plan just be sure you aren't paying too much for maintenance fees.

Out of all of the places I have worked, WorldMark by Wyndham and the Jockey Club have the least expensive fees. There are also resorts in Mexico where you only pay maintenance on the years you use the program, but I don't really advise owning real estate in Mexico if you can get the same thing here and just trade into those wonderful places. Keep in mind, even if the maintenance fees rise, you are going to be staying in condos instead of hotel rooms and most people feel the extra money for the extra space and luxury is worth it. By utilizing the kitchen for one meal a day, you can offset a majority of your costs.

What part of the country do you or will you live in?

You can trade your timeshare to over six thousand resorts scattered throughout every country, but it is generally not the easiest thing to do, even with the tricks I teach. There are also costs every time you go through an exchange company, and you may not want to pay that on top of what you already are paying. The list of resort developers I previously mentioned also notes which region each company is best suited for, so take some time to find a company that has multiple locations or properties in places you would like to go a majority of the time. Having an ownership with many different options will give you a much higher satisfaction rate. Having to trade every time you want to take a short trip can be difficult and expensive.

How often do you want to travel?

There are two things I think you should look at when deciding to buy a vacation ownership package. The first thing is to decide if you are interested in renting some of your time out to offset your fees, or are you going to use the credits for all of your own travel (air, car, cruise, etc.)? If you are going to be doing more than just staying in condos, then buy enough points for all your traveling needs. If you are just buying to stay in the rooms, then I would recommend buying less than you are currently using. Never buy exactly what you need; buy a slightly smaller program and stretch it into what you want or need.

Example 1: *You and your wife travel one week a year in the summer, then take one or two mini trips per year. Buy enough points for a two-bedroom at a prime resort. Use a one-bedroom week worth of points for your big trip, and utilize the left-over points and possibly a little bonus time instead of buying two weeks.*

Example 2: *You take one week a year plus a few mini trips and you would like to pay nothing in maintenance and maybe make a little money. Buy two or more weeks and utilize one for your vacation needs and one to rent out and make money.*

Example 3: *You vacation several times a year and take mini trips throughout; you fly a couple of times of year and take an occasional cruise. In this case, become a VIP member with one of the major developers and buy* *enough points to cover all of those trips. This way, when you retire, you can still travel the same way and have everything paid for.*

The key is to not spend money unnecessarily and have a program big enough to fit your needs. It's also nice having extra points in case you would like to stay in larger rooms like penthouses from time to time. Points based systems really allow you to focus your energies on exactly what you are using without requiring any extra work. You can also roll your points over a year and borrow a year ahead for any large vacations you may have. With most points programs, this allows you to utilize up to three years of points at one time. Just remember to do a little research, get a game plan, and buy what is appropriate for your family. The nice thing about points is you can start small and increase as necessary when the timing and budget are right.

Mini-trips vs. long vacations

I don't think there is much to be said regarding long or short vacations when it comes to ownership. In nearly every case you are most likely better off with a points program, which gives you the choice of either length of stay. In the rare case there is a certain resort or area you would like to go and you don't mind always staying for a week, then buying an old deeded timeshare week could be worth it. If there is a certain place you like to go, it's always best to buy a week at that resort to avoid hassles when booking, especially since you can trade nightly through nearly all of the major exchange companies with either your points or deeded weeks. Some developers, like Blugreen, will also have a way for you to turn your program into RCI points. If you have RCI points, you can utilize them for condos, hotels, airfare, car rentals, and many other options.

When you only go on short notice trips for a few nights, it is especially important for you to do some homework. Some developers are restrictive as far as getting good reservations on weekends and holidays, and some programs are disastrous as well as expensive for short notice travelers.

What quality of resorts do you want to stay in?

As I have previously said, you don't have to stay at the Four Seasons to have a good time, but for the same price as a three-star resort, why not stay at the nicest place possible? If you are staying in three- or four-star hotels then all of the above-mentioned resort developers will be adequate for your needs. If, on the other hand, you like to stay at five-star resorts, then choose one of the higher-end brands. In most all cases, the major timeshare brands are equal to or better than your average hotel room, so just go with the one that best suits your needs and buy the cheapest timeshare you can find. In the case of five-star resorts, find the one that best suits your needs in the areas you like and make sure you get points. The higher-end timeshares have much to offer as far as affiliations with the many hotel chains. The Starwood vacation ownership group (Westin), Marriott, Hilton, Wyndham and Diamond resort groups are known for offering a multitude of options when staying at hotels as well. Timeshares will not cover 100 percent of your vacation needs, and in these cases it is good to belong to a company that gives large discounts on hotel stays and everything else.

The big question: buy a resale or buy from the developers?

I don't believe there is a bad timeshare deal from any of the major developers. I can hear it now: people are going to say, "Oh that's because he works in the industry," but I honestly do believe this. Buying from the secondary market will always be cheaper, but sometimes the benefits do not transfer over, which could end up costing you more in the long run. The only time it is a bad deal is if you can't afford it or you don't use it. If you buy a timeshare and you don't use it, there is absolutely no right or wrong way to buy.

Buying from the developer

If you buy airline tickets, take cruises and like tour packages, then buying from the developers is the best way to go. The reason is most major developers make it as difficult as possible to use the full benefits of the program if you didn't buy it from them. For most developers, you cannot combine credits or weeks with the other credits or weeks you own unless, in some cases you upgrade directly with them at some point. The major developers have created programs that will save you more money on travel then you would have saved buying a timeshare on the secondary market. According to AAA, if you spend $2,500 a year with a 10 to 15 percent average increase in costs, you will spend over $45,000 in fifteen years. If this is the case, then you will be perfectly fine buying from the developer. If you can use your credits or points for every kind of travel, you are definitely going to spend less money than you would otherwise.

If you do buy a timeshare from the developer, I believe your best bet is to buy a small package up front, and then upgrade it at a later date. Most developers give owners lower prices after they have bought in because the marketing costs are lower. Do not buy the absolute lowest package, though, as in most cases they are not the best deals, having the least amount of time and usually the highest maintenance fees. When buying from the developer, always ask the salesperson if there is anything else he or she can throw in the deal for you, like bonus points, extra weeks, or show tickets and dinner. It is just like buying a car: they always hold a little something back to throw in; so make sure to hold out as long as you can. Buying from the developers is not a bad deal if you are going to use your package for all of your vacation needs, as it will save you thousands over traditional vacationing. The biggest benefit of buying from the developers is you will have the ability to use all of what you own with the full use of their programs and VIP benefits, when applicable. If you buy timeshares off of the secondary market, most resorts won't let you combine them together and they won't allow you to use VIP benefits or certain parts of their programs. Really weigh the cost savings of buying on the secondary market against having to buy airfare, cruises, rental cars and hotels for the rest of your life. To figure this amount, take your travel costs over a 15-year period, adding 10 to 15 percent per year for inflation.

As always, you can go to the Timeshare Users Group and ask questions of others on the subject or contact my offices and we can assist you. There is an application called iTimeshare (iPhone) that will allow you to calculate out what you spend with inflation for your travel. I am sure you can Google how to calculate your vacation costs over a period of time and find the right site as well.

Buying a resale

As far as great deals are concerned, timeshare re-sales are the best for the value the industry offers. If you buy a used timeshare, you will be paying on average only 10 to 50 percent of what the developer charges. This doesn't mean resales are not as valuable; it is just the marketing and sales costs on the primary market are tremendous. It is no different from buying a car from the dealer compared to someone off of Craigslist. Typically, you are going to get a better deal because you don't have to pay for the huge building, advertising, and sales commissions. There are some limitations to buying a resale, as I mentioned earlier, but as far as overall value, they are worth every penny in most cases.

The developers are well aware of the resale market, and every year each company is and will continue to make it difficult to use resales with their programs. Some developers will restrict you from utilizing credits, points, or weeks with their extra programs.

Example 1: *If you buy WorldMark by Wyndham points from anyone other than an immediate relative after November 2006, you cannot combine them with a program you already own and they are not Travel Share eligible. You also cannot use the points toward qualifying as a VIP.*

In the WorldMark by Wyndham program, the VIP levels and the Travel Share program will allow you to triple the power of your points, giving you multiple vacations out of just one week. The program also gives you the ability to use your points for cruises, car rentals, houses, airline tickets, and many other things. If you buy a resale, you will lose those advantages, so analyze whether paying more for credits up front from the developer will be less than a lifetime of travel costs. This cost of travel expenses year after year is more than you think, so be very careful of fooling yourself with the low upfront cost of a resale.

Example 2: *You buy a deeded week from the Marriott on the resale market. You are not automatically enrolled into the Marriott's customer loyalty program.*

Resale companies say you can join the program later for free, but I would check into that to be sure. The Marriott's loyalty program also lets you trade your weeks for points that can be exchanged for a myriad of vacation opportunities including cruises, airfare, hotel stays, dining vouchers, golf packages and more.

Whenever you buy a timeshare resale, there are some things you should do to protect yourself. Also remember to do your homework.

Things to research:

1. Call the developer of the resort you are thinking of purchasing and ask them as many question as you can.

   a. What is the difference if I don't buy from you?

   b. How much do I have to pay to transfer the title?

   c. Is the owner's account in good standing and paid off? (They might not give you this personal information)

   d. How many credits or weeks is it?

   e. Can I take a tour of the resort or attend a sales presentation?

2. Find out from the timeshare resale company or owner:

   a. Are the maintenance fees up to date?

b. Are there any banked weeks or points with RCI?

c. Does the resort get special assessments in addition to the maintenance fees?

d. Does he or she have the owner's manual, resort directory, and RCI/II books to give you?

Also make sure to use a legitimate escrow company to handle the transaction. The escrow companies will provide:

- Preparation of deed and state tax forms; this ensures all applicable taxes are dealt with and no hidden costs appear down the road

- Delivery of closing documents to buyer and seller, reviewed by an attorney

- Delivery of deed to clerk of court; this means the papers are taken to county clerk for recording

- Escrow of purchasing money funds; this money is held in escrow until closing

- Acquisition of Estoppel certificate; this is a notice detailing any ongoing outstanding costs, such as maintenance fees, taxes, special assessments, and when the next period is due

- Resort notification of transfer; this is written notification of the transfer of the recorded deed delivered to resort

- Transfer of ownership: transfer of title from the seller to the buyer

If you are buying a point's ownership off of someone who doesn't have a deed attached to it, there will be considerably less paperwork. In most points situations you won't need to use a closing company just to fill out the transfer paperwork from the resort. In points programs you are simply buying a piece of a trust, so think of it as purchasing a stock in the company. Since it is not actual real estate, there is not as much paperwork.

As far as being a buyer on the secondary market, you are relatively safe from being scammed, but still do your best due diligence on the company you are dealing with or with the person from whom you are going to buy.

The best places to find great timeshare resale's at the lowest cost through reputable companies are:

www.tug2.net

www.redweek.com

www.ebay.com

These are the top three sites I would start with because you are buying directly from the seller in most cases. In cases where there are no weeks or points for sale where you would like to travel, your next best bet is to buy from a resale company. For a list of the best resale companies, refer to my list of companies that are recommended by people who have actually used them in the chapter on how to sell your timeshare.

When dealing with these resale companies, keep in mind they are usually willing to negotiate down the price they are asking, so always start with an offer lower then they advertise. There are hundreds of these companies out there with tons of inventory from every developer in the world. Just figure out which program you want to buy and Google it. The list of companies willing to sell that company will be endless. Check whether or not the company has a good record with the Better Business Bureau. It should also be a member of American Resort Development Association (ARDA) as well. The ARDA exists to protect timeshare owners, so that is a very important symbol to have on the company's website. When you find one you think is good, you can also start a discussion at the Timeshares Users Group to see what everyone else is saying about that particular company.

A lot of people prefer to purchase from the resort to have the peace of mind of knowing who they are dealing with and because the resort can usually throw in enough gifts to offset the cost. Don't forget, the resorts are very powerful and provide a great product at a great price with an average break-even point of about ten years. They also have deep pockets and affiliations that can give you gifts worth many thousands of dollars. This makes the savings on the secondary market not worth as much in some cases.

No matter which option you chose for buying your first or fortieth timeshare, you will typically not get a bad deal with any developer if you are already traveling. Just make sure to always do your homework, ask a lot of questions, and always ask for a deal.

Chapter Ten

Conclusion of timeshare education

Timeshare is a wonderful industry that has provided families with extraordinary experiences they might not have otherwise had. With costs rising every year, most of us probably wouldn't have been able to afford these trips otherwise. Owning a timeshare allows you to have these experiences time and time again, year after year, from a one-time purchase. If you do the things I taught you in the book, you can also make maintenance fees a non-issue. The industry is far from perfect. Many of the developers are fairly small with limited resources in their programs. As the industry grows and the major developers bring more innovative products to the market, your program will continue to grow in value.

Any program will bring you much use and happiness if you simply understand the principles of how things work. You can use your timeshare to create unbelievable memories, as a source for a little extra income, or as a tool to barter with. The secondary market is tough to navigate and there are so many scams and unscrupulous people out there that you must do research whenever dealing with a company on the resale end. No matter what situation you are currently facing with your vacation ownership plan, there are options for you.

If you would like to get updated information on the industry as well as tips on how to better use your program, get *Timesharing Today,* the magazine. This has been a top industry publication for many years and can help you with its great articles no matter which developers you own with. These articles include information such as which resorts are pet-friendly and where you go to find them (www. petfriendlytimeshares.com). There are many articles such as new tricks on how to get the resorts you want as well as reviews on those resorts. *Timesharing Today* also has articles from top industry experts discussing the future of the industry and new opportunities. Another great publication I like is *Perspective Magazine,* which covers both the timeshare and fractional markets. They have fantastic interviews with the top CEOs in the industry and give fabulous insight into the upcoming places and events released into the market. Due to the mix of resort styles, as a timeshare owner you can see and access beautiful fractional homes and condos that most timeshare owners don't even know exist. Reading this publication will give you access to the most exquisite residences in the world, most of which are available with your current program. If you are a global traveler, you will also enjoy this magazine because of its focus on international travel.

The timeshare industry is a vast network of opportunities and choices, and hopefully this book has enlightened you on how to better use your program. If you ever think there is something you can't do or a reservation you can't get, refer back to this book for tips and strategies that will last a lifetime.

I would like to thank you for buying my book and for the time we have spent together. May the rest of your life be filled with many great travel memories!

The end

Made in the USA
Charleston, SC
20 April 2012